Optimizing Foreign Military Sales Roles, Responsibilities, and Authorities

LISA SAUM-MANNING, JEFFERSON P. MARQUIS, IRINA A. CHINDEA, DANIEL ELINOFF, THEILINE PIGOTT, ELLIOTT BRENNAN

Prepared for the Defense Security Cooperation Agency
Approved for public release; distribution is unlimited

RAND NATIONAL SECURITY RESEARCH DIVISION

For more information on this publication, visit **www.rand.org/t/RRA2631-1**.

About RAND

The RAND Corporation is a research organization that develops solutions to public policy challenges to help make communities throughout the world safer and more secure, healthier and more prosperous. RAND is nonprofit, nonpartisan, and committed to the public interest. To learn more about RAND, visit www.rand.org.

Research Integrity

Our mission to help improve policy and decisionmaking through research and analysis is enabled through our core values of quality and objectivity and our unwavering commitment to the highest level of integrity and ethical behavior. To help ensure our research and analysis are rigorous, objective, and nonpartisan, we subject our research publications to a robust and exacting quality-assurance process; avoid both the appearance and reality of financial and other conflicts of interest through staff training, project screening, and a policy of mandatory disclosure; and pursue transparency in our research engagements through our commitment to the open publication of our research findings and recommendations, disclosure of the source of funding of published research, and policies to ensure intellectual independence. For more information, visit www.rand.org/about/principles.

Published by the RAND Corporation, Santa Monica, Calif.

Library of Congress Cataloging-in-Publication Data is available for this publication.
ISBN: 978-1-9774-1330-7

Cover: Cydney Lee/U.S. Air Force.

About This Report

This report assesses how the complex array of roles, responsibilities, and authorities that shape the Foreign Military Sales (FMS) process are first defined in policy and related guidance and then implemented in practice by a diverse range of stakeholder organizations at strategic, operational, and tactical levels of execution. The research reveals that the leading security assistance (SA) organizations lack adequate powers to hold relevant stakeholder organizations accountable for expediting the FMS process. Even where these powers do exist, these organizations sometimes fail to fully leverage them. Additionally, the report describes unclear, conflicting, missing, and overlapping roles and responsibilities among entities at the operational (implementing agencies) and tactical (security cooperation organizations [SCO]) levels. Stakeholders assert that as a result, the FMS process can struggle to live up to its commitments in a timely fashion, posing risks to U.S. partners' abilities to build critical military capabilities and capacities and potentially U.S. relationships with these partners. The research reported here was completed in February 2024 and underwent security review with the sponsor and the Defense Office of Prepublication and Security Review before public release.

RAND National Security Research Division

This research was sponsored by the Defense Security Cooperation Agency (DSCA) and conducted within the International Security and Defense Policy Program of the RAND National Security Research Division (NSRD), which operates the National Defense Research Institute (NDRI), a federally funded research and development center sponsored by the Office of the Secretary of Defense (OSD), the Joint Staff, the Unified Combatant Commands, the U.S. Navy, the U.S. Marine Corps, the defense agencies, and the defense intelligence enterprise.

Acknowledgments

We thank Payce Carupella and Heather Meyer from DSCA for their support throughout each phase of this research. We also appreciate the more than 100 security cooperation stakeholders who volunteered their time to share their experiences and perspectives regarding a wide range of FMS activities. Each stakeholder shed light on an important piece of an incredibly complex puzzle. We further extend our gratitude to former director of the Defense Security Corporation, Lieutenant General (retired) Charles W. Hooper, and Jennifer Moroney of RAND for their meticulous reviews of this report.

Summary

In June 2022, U.S. Secretary of Defense (SECDEF) Lloyd Austin directed the Department of Defense (DoD) to identify potential improvements to the delivery of defense capabilities to international security partners through the Foreign Military Sales (FMS) system. The FMS Tiger Team co-led by the Deputy Under Secretary for Policy and the Under Secretary of Defense for Acquisition and Sustainment (USD(A&S)) identified specific challenges within the FMS system and proposed solutions to improve capability delivery to allies and partners aligned to strategic outcomes sought by the National Defense Strategy. The study revealed that, among many other issues, roles, responsibilities, and authorities (RRA) issues can contribute to timeliness and efficiency problems. As a result, the Deputy Secretary of Defense directed the Defense Security Cooperation Agency (DSCA) to sponsor a RAND Corporation and National Defense Research Institute study aimed at (1) articulating how RRA challenges impede the FMS process and (2) developing recommendations to address them.

Senior DoD policy officials advised early on in our research what they viewed as the most vexing challenges pertaining to FMS-related RRAs. The preponderance of concerns centered on the perception that "there is this gaping hole in transparency and authority when it comes to FMS"[1] and that "success looks like a clear delineation of what each of the stakeholders' RRAs are at each stage of the process."[2] Determining who has (or should have) authority and responsibility over what duties and visibility into what phases was only one challenge highlighted. Stakeholders also expressed concerns that RRAs are sometimes competing or conflicting, unclear or missing, or duplicative or inefficient. These problems ultimately pose risks to U.S. efforts to build partner relationships and the capabilities and capacities of foreign militaries.

This report aims to explore and, where possible, offer clarity and recommendations pertaining to the following questions:

- **What are the authorities in the FMS process?**
- **Where are the gaps in RRAs?**
- **What actions could be taken to overcome these challenges?**

To answer these questions, we conducted an extensive desk review of the laws, policies, authorities, and related guidance that govern the process to gain a baseline understanding of *how FMS functions on paper.* We also reviewed past reform efforts and held interviews with over 100 FMS stakeholders with over 1,300 work years of collective experience within the security assistance (SA) community to gain insight into *how the process actually works in practice.*

---

1 DSCA stakeholder, interview with the authors, March 2, 2023; security cooperation office (SCO) personnel, interview with the authors, April 28, 2023.

2 DoD policy official, interview with the authors, May 2, 2023.

For policy- and strategic-level perspectives, we spoke with policy- and strategic-level organizations, specifically the Office of the Secretary of Defense—Policy (OSD-P), the Office of the Under Secretary of Defense for Acquisition and Sustainment (OUSD(A&S)), the Office of the Under Secretary of Defense for Research and Engineering (OUSD(R&E)), the Joint Staff, and the Department of State (DoS). At the nexus of strategic and operational levels of FMS activities, we spoke with stakeholders from DSCA and the Defense Technology and Security Administration (DTSA). We also spoke with operational stakeholders at each of the service implementing agencies (IAs) and geographic combatant commands (CCMDs) whose missions are, or potentially could be, affected by military partners' abilities to acquire U.S. defense equipment through FMS acquisitions. For frontline or what we consider tactical-level insights, we interviewed personnel from several SCOs working within CCMD areas of responsibility. Figure S.1 illustrates our approach.

Our research revealed that FMS plays a vital part in enhancing partner military capabilities. However, various factors can hinder stakeholder organizations from executing FMS processes and commitments promptly. One obstacle is DoD's hesitation to view allies, partners, and the SA provided through FMS as vital components of its contingency planning for warfare. Establishing an effective and efficient FMS process necessitates a cultural recognition of the valuable contributions that capable allies and partners, facilitated by the acquisition of U.S. defense equipment, bring to the battlefield.

Despite some reluctance among military planners to fully embrace their contributions, FMS demand has increased in recent years, and the security assistance community is under

FIGURE S.1

RAND Approach to Assessing Foreign Military Sales Challenges Regarding Roles, Responsibilities, and Authorities

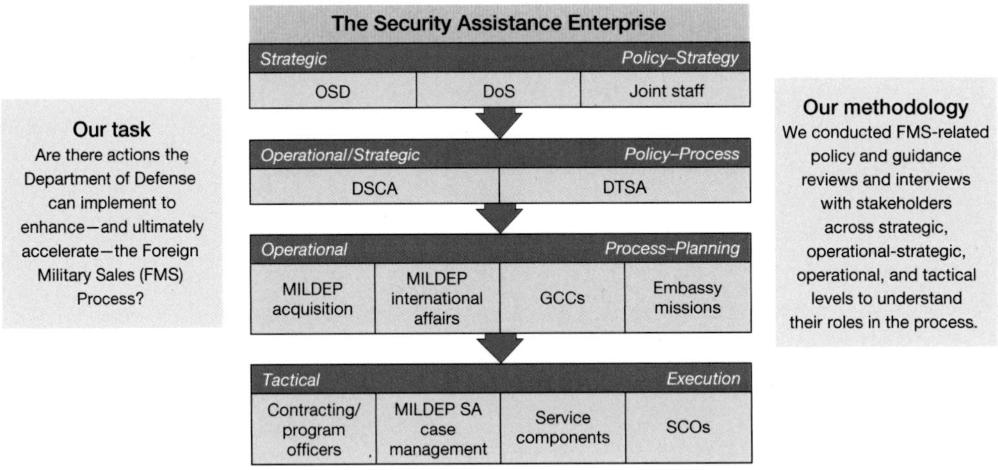

NOTE: DoS = Department of State; GCC = Geographic Combatant Command; MILDEP = Military Department; OSD = Office of the Secretary of Defense; SA = security assistance.

pressure to deliver more quickly on major cases. Frustrations reverberate across the workforce during all phases of the process, from senior-level leaders who struggle to exert the authorities required to direct and administer FMS, to frontline personnel tasked to support those requirements. Some of the challenges stem from the design of a process that involves many touchpoints across different stakeholder organizations that do not fall under a clear chain of command in the context of the FMS process, making it difficult for any one of these organizations to have authority over or visibility into the details of FMS cases as they move (or fail to move) through the various phases of the process.

It is important to note that our study team also encountered issues with accessing certain types of data, namely data on FMS case delivery timelines,[3] which made it impossible to independently quantify and thus verify the delays and potential implications of implementing such a system under the current constellation of RRAs. Nevertheless, the consensus concern is that delays in processing FMS cases may create risks to partner military's capability requirements and, subsequently, U.S. relationships with these partners.

The following section summarizes our key findings and recommendations.

Key Findings

Key Finding 1: The Defense Security Cooperation Agency Lacks Sufficient Authorities to Direct the Foreign Military Sales Implementation Process and to Hold Suborganizations Accountable

In many cases, we found that authorities and guidance exist on paper but do not go far enough to enable optimal oversight and enforcement program requirements. For example, DoD Directive 5105.65 grants DSCA the authority over FMS administrative funds, and in theory those funds could be pulled back in situations where a case has gone wayward. Yet, in practice, one DSCA stakeholder noted that "the power of the purse is fool's gold."[4] Limiting funds might lead to shortages in manpower or other critical resources and ultimately further impede the very process the agency aims to optimize.

During the initial phase of our research (January 2023), DSCA lacked administrative control over SCO personnel playing a central role in facilitating the relationships, processes, and activities required for successful FMS cases.[5] However, as of February 2023, DoD leadership

---

[3] Although DSCA does collect timeline-related case development data (Letter of Request to implemented Letter of Agreement), it does not have regular access to specific information on the status of FMS cases in case execution phases (implemented Letter of Agreement to contract and contract to delivery).

[4] DSCA official, interview with the authors, May 11, 2023.

[5] FMS in many countries is just a small piece of the SCO's overall roles and responsibilities. Some countries have a negligible FMS portfolio, but they are important players when it comes to operational activities. Besides FMS, SCOs are involved in representational events, personnel exchange programs, exercises, international military education and training, key leader engagements, crisis response, and many other activities in which DSCA is not involved but over which the CCMD has oversight.

granted DSCA increased administrative authority over SCO personnel.[6] At the time of this writing (February 2024), the details of administrative and operational controls of SCO personnel are still being worked out between OSD, DSCA, the CCMDs, and the services. This includes potential modifications to DSCA's RRAs as they relate to the SCO workforce in the Department of Defense Directives (DoDDs) that establish authority, assign responsibilities, and provide guidance for the conduct of DoD activities.

Additionally, DSCA lacks the authority to hold service IA officials accountable for failing to meet case development timelines and standards and to keep it apprised of problems related to major FMS proposals and cases. DSCA similarly lacks the authority to require MILDEP contracting and acquisition officials to provide periodic updates on the status of security assistance–related cases.

Recommendation 1: Amend Department of Defense Directives and Service Regulations to Give the Defense Security Cooperation Agency Enforcement Authority in Areas It Is Responsible for Overseeing and Managing

Our first series of recommendations center on amendments to DoDDs and service regulations to give DSCA enforcement authority in areas it is responsible for overseeing and managing. This includes amending directives to reflect the transfer of SCO personnel to DSCA's administrative control for training purposes before taking up their assignments and giving DSCA approving authority over all SCO personnel billet descriptions and, where appropriate (i.e., SCOs conducting significant security cooperation activities), SCO chief selections. DSCA will also recommend FMS-related criteria that should be addressed in all SCO chief evaluations.

The recommendation also includes amending DoDDs to institute the development of reporting standards and procedures for MILDEP security assistance–related production and evaluating MILDEP reports for accuracy and timeliness. Additionally, DSCA should be given the authority to establish a data czar position with the mandate to facilitate transparency through data sharing across the FMS enterprise.

[6] DSCA gained the authority for administrative, not operational, control over SCO personnel via the Secretary of Defense (SECDEF)–signed National Defense Strategy Implementation (NDS-I) Task 4.5.1 on February 7, 2023. The Office of the Secretary of the Air Force International Affairs (SAF/IA) previously nonconcurred with DSCA taking operational control of SCO personnel, and it was agreed and stated in the NDS-I that operational control will remain with the CCMDs, with DSCA having administrative control over SCO personnel. U.S. Department of Defense, *National Defense Strategy Implementation: DOD Workforce Needed to Build Capacity of Allies and Partners. Task 4.5.1—Report and Action Plan*, February 7, 2023, unclassified document provided by the sponsor and not publicly available.

Key Finding 2: Leading Security Assistance Organizations Could Undertake Additional Responsibilities Related to Foreign Military Sales

Stakeholders at all levels of command and activities have expressed the need for additional guidance. FMS is a security assistance program and therefore falls under the jurisdiction of DoS, yet DoS is often absent from key decision points when FMS stakeholders need guidance the most. OSD-P struggles to crystallize its FMS responsibilities, leading to missed opportunities to streamline competing priorities, reduce confusion, and elevate awareness of how FMS supports U.S. foreign policy and military objectives.

Recommendation 2: The Department of State and Department of Defense Should Identify, Clarify, and Codify Additional Responsibilities for Managing Foreign Military Sales Requirements

To address these issues, DoD and DoS need to establish and formalize additional roles in managing FMS requirements. To this end, DoS (in consultation with OSD-P or DSCA) should establish and articulate clear partner prioritization requirements annually that align with foreign policy objectives to ensure a coordinated approach to FMS.[7] While we are aware of previous attempts to establish strategic-level security sector assistance and security cooperation prioritization guidance,[8] we believe that the current disconnect between FMS supply and demand merits DoS and DoD leaders' revisitation of this issue to overcome long-standing barriers to collaboration on practical guidelines as to what capabilities are needed most and what partners are most important to the United States from a security assistance perspective over the midterm. DoS could also contribute more to FMS training and education opportunities to alleviate any confusion among personnel regarding their Title 22 roles and responsibilities.

Additionally, we propose extending Under Secretary of Defense for Policy (USD(P)) authority to establish and articulate DoD strategic guidance pertaining to FMS. DSCA would then lead in developing a systematic FMS case prioritization framework. This framework could play an important role in informing and supporting decisions regarding the prioritization of FMS deliveries and provide better alignment of priorities among FMS stakeholders within DoD and across DoS and DoD. USD(P) should also promote greater interagency collaboration by mandating the attendance of regional desks at these events.

---

[7] Although DoD operational objectives do not always align perfectly with DoS priorities, the interagency Integrated Country Strategy is a common guiding document on which DoD relies.

[8] Presidential Policy Directive 23, *Fact Sheet: U.S. Security Sector Assistance Policy*, White House, 2013. See also Christopher Paul, Michael Nixon, Heather Peterson, Beth Grill, and Jessica Yeats, *The RAND Security Cooperation Prioritization and Propensity Matching Tool,* RAND Corporation, TL-112-OSD, November 6, 2013.

When FMS purchases are deemed the appropriate sourcing solution, USD(P) should also become a more assertive advocate for their value and potential contributions in meeting U.S. national security objectives. Opportunities might include systematically encouraging CCMDs to incorporate capabilities acquired through FMS by partner nations into their contingency planning, tabletop exercises, and other relevant activities that support the needs of the warfighter.[9]

Key Finding 3: Implementing Organizations Also Lack Line Authority to Compel Action from Acquisition Community Partners

Each MILDEP serves as an implementing organization responsible for carrying out critical aspects of the FMS program. At the apex of the loosely connected security assistance structures within the services are SAF/IA, the Deputy Assistant Secretary of the Army for Defense Exports and Cooperation (DASA (DE&C)), and the Navy International Programs Office (NIPO). Although these organizations have distinct configurations, command structures, and roles, they share similar challenges and authorities with DSCA and OSD in terms of lacking the ability to compel case management organizations that fall outside their "line authority"[10] to provide visibility into a range of FMS implementation activities.[11] This is of particular concern with respect to their ability to gain visibility into security assistance activities of the MILDEP acquisition organizations and procurement timelines from relevant defense industry partners.

Recommendation 3: Amend Department of Defense Directives and Service Regulations to Give Leading Department of Defense Security Assistance Organizations Enforcement Authority in Areas They Are Responsible for Overseeing and Managing

To increase the chance for accurate, timely reporting of FMS case execution activities, we propose that DoDDs be amended to state that OUSD(A&S) has the responsibility and authority to develop enhanced reporting standards and procedures for acquisition contracting and production, including for FMS cases. Furthermore, we recommend that OUSD(A&S) be given the responsibility and authority to periodically evaluate MILDEP contracting and pro-

[9] One Navy IA stakeholder did note that foreign partners' FMS-built capabilities are already factored into bilateral and multilateral training exercises in the U.S. Southern Command area of responsibility. This was the only interviewee who mentioned it. There likely are other examples where this is occurring, though perhaps not on a systematic basis.

[10] *Line authority* describes a centralized process with a clear chain of command whereby top managers oversee the activities of middle managers and middle managers direct the activities of line workers.

[11] An alternative possible explanation is that this situation could be due to broken processes and personalities or relationship issues rather than lack of authority. However, both our review of existing authorities and the interviews we conducted support the finding that it is a lack of authority.

duction for accuracy and timeliness. This visibility is crucial for (1) establishing a system of accountability, (2) ensuring that personnel adhere to standards and guidelines, and (3) identifying strengths and areas for process improvements.

Key Finding 4: Duplicative Roles, Particularly in the Army Foreign Military Sales Enterprise, Further Impede the Foreign Military Sales Process

During our interviews, a recurring concern that emerged was the potential for friction within the FMS process due to duplicative roles and responsibilities. We delved into guidance to further investigate this claim and determined that, while there are a multitude of stakeholders, most of their roles and responsibilities are adequately discreet and that redundancy is not an impediment to case delivery timelines. However, there are certain circumstances where similarities among these roles can cloud and slow the process, and this is seen most often in Army FMS cases: Stakeholders contend that an overly complex case management structure exists between multiple chains of command, creating complex communication channels and a lack of central authority.

Recommendation 4: Improve Clarity on Operational-Level Roles and Responsibilities; the Army Should Explore Organizational Restructuring Options to Reduce Duplication

The Army is currently undergoing a significant review of its FMS enterprise. While we have not been privy to these discussions, our independent assessment is that the Army should consider amending guidance to clarify the language used to describe its case management roles and consider reallocating and realigning some RRAs to reduce complexity.

Some of our recommendations may be easier to implement than others; some may stand to have more impact than others; still others might not be worth the trade-offs. For recommendations pertaining to DSCA in particular, it might be worth submitting them to SECDEF and the Deputy Secretary of Defense in an action memo and allowing key stakeholders to add their perspectives before the package goes up for formal consideration. This would surface issues to enable informed decisionmaking and give DSCA an opportunity to work through potential concerns. Some recommendations could be implemented as "pilots," which should enable greater data gathering on the actual benefits and trade-offs.

Contents

Figures and Tables

Figures

Tables

CHAPTER 1

Introduction

Foreign Military Sales (FMS) is a process, authorized by the Arms Export Control Act, through which the U.S. government transfers defense articles, services, and training to international partners and organizations. The FMS program is funded by administrative charges to foreign purchasers and is operated at no cost to taxpayers. The Defense Security Cooperation Agency (DSCA) administers the FMS program for the U.S. Department of Defense (DoD). Under FMS, the U.S. government uses DoD's acquisition system to procure defense articles and services on behalf of its partners. Eligible countries may purchase defense articles and services with their own funds or with funds provided through U.S. government–sponsored assistance programs. In certain cases, defense articles may be obtained through grants or leases.[1]

FMS is also a critical U.S. foreign policy tool. It plays an integral role in achieving U.S. national security goals outlined in the 2022 National Defense Strategy, as enhancing our allies' and partners' military capabilities and capacities features prominently in maintaining an effective integrated deterrent posture against U.S. adversaries.[2] With an average of over $44 billion in sales,[3] the program is also a key source of revenue for the U.S. defense industry.

Yet, the FMS program has faced long-standing criticism for failing to meet both U.S. and partner expectations. Mismatches between U.S. weapons systems and partners' capabilities to employ and sustain them are a frequent complaint, as is the seemingly glacial pace of delivery. Critical assessments of the FMS process warn that an ineffective process contributes to the perception of a wavering U.S. commitment to allies and partners that in turn provides an opening for America's adversaries and strategic competitors to exploit.[4]

---

[1] For additional information, see Defense Security Cooperation Agency, "Foreign Military Sales FAQ," website, undated. See also Department of Defense Joint Publication 3-20, *Security Cooperation*, Joint Chiefs of Staff, 2022, Chapter II-5.

[2] U.S. Department of Defense, *National Defense Strategy of the United States of America*, 2022.

[3] Office of the Spokesperson, "FMS 2023: Retooling Foreign Military Sales for An Age of Strategic Competition: Fact Sheet," U.S. Department of State, May 18, 2023.

[4] Michael Kurilla, "Statement for the Record General Michael 'Erik' Kurilla Commander, U.S. Central Command Before the Senate Armed Services Committee on the Posture of U.S. Central Command," U.S. Central Command, March 13, 2023.

Previous Foreign Military Sales Reform Efforts

Over the last five years alone, there have been numerous DoD efforts and initiatives of varying scope to reform and reorganize U.S. security cooperation, including proposed changes to the FMS process. Many aspects of these previous reform efforts related to large, intractable problems within FMS, such as anticipating partner demands,[5] facilitating interagency coordination,[6] and improving the domestic-based acquisition process on which the FMS process is built. Recommendations pertained to issues such as enhancing workforce training and development, enhancing Technology Security and Foreign Disclosure (TSFD) requirements analysis, streamlining processes within FMS cases such as prioritization among cases, and increasing oversight and transparency.

Some of these efforts focused on issues that continued to emerge during our study, suggesting that the system has struggled to enact change regarding long-standing problems. One area has been reforms to workforce training and development to professionalize critical roles in the FMS process. In 2010, the Security Cooperation Reform Task Force (SCRTF) recommended creating a certification curriculum for FMS professionals similar to the curriculum for the Defense Acquisition Workforce. Vision 2020, drawn up in 2014, sought to identify key skills and certificates required for each position and then develop a mechanism to track workforce certification. In 2015, the FMS Improvements effort, which was led by the director of DSCA, implemented the reforms proposed by the SCRTF and incorporated FMS training into the Defense Acquisition University curriculum. Furthermore, in response to the requirements of the fiscal year (FY) 2017 National Defense Authorization Act (NDAA), "the Secretary of Defense directed DSCA to establish the Security Cooperation Workforce Development Program and lead the Department's education, training, and certification program per 10 USC, Section §384."[7] As a result, DSCA stood up the Defense Security Cooperation University (DSCU) in September 2019 with the aim "to support its requirement to train, certify, and provide for the long-term development of the security cooperation workforce at home and abroad."[8]

Another focus area of previous efforts relevant to this report is prioritization of cases in the FMS process. The SCRTF, Presidential Policy Directive 23,[9] and the FY17 NDAA all included recommendations for streamlining communications and decisions across the FMS process. The SCRTF recommended establishing DoD-wide "Equipping Priority Guidelines" that define DoD's priorities for equipping both the U.S. and partner nation forces, and to direct the Security Cooperation Steering Group to oversee high-priority or urgent FMS cases.

---

[5] Anticipating delays that emanate from partner nation processes can be an additional challenge.

[6] Congressional notifications, while out of scope for this report, are an example of a coordination process that can further slow FMS deliveries.

[7] Defense Security Cooperation University, "History," website, undated.

[8] Defense Security Cooperation University, undated.

[9] Presidential Policy Directive 23, 2013.

Similarly, Presidential Policy Directive 23 established an interagency security assistance roundtable to encourage collaboration and FMS policy cohesion. The FY17 NDAA mandated that DoD and the U.S. Department of State (DoS) issue joint mechanisms for policy, planning, and implementation of FMS.

In addition to internal efforts by DoD, the FMS process has been subject to review and reform through reports to Congress by the U.S. Government Accountability Office (GAO). The earliest such report, titled *Foreign Military Sales: A Growing Concern*, was issued in 1976 and identified issues within the FMS process that persist today, including concerns around technology security, sustainment of systems sold to partner nations, and the impact of FMS on the readiness and capabilities of U.S. forces. In recent years, GAO reports related to the FMS process have been issued on improving timeliness and other performance metrics, streamlining the review process for FMS cases across the interagency and Congress, and strengthening financial oversight. Since 2018, there have been four recommendations by GAO that are all related to DSCA's policy for handling administrative costs. These recommendations establish a process and give the director of DSCA authority to review administrative costs of Military Departments (MILDEPs) involved in FMS cases, which empowers DSCA with some oversight capability for the FMS process.

There have also been over 20 RAND Corporation studies focused on aspects of security cooperation that encompass the FMS process since 2008.[10] These studies have assessed and offered recommendations on aspects such as authorities and planning; activities aimed at building partner capacity, security force assistance, and interoperability; methods of assessing, monitoring, and evaluating security cooperation activities; and lessons learned and best practices. These previous reform efforts by DoD, GAO, and RAND have sought to reform the security cooperation tools and processes to better meet the needs of operational commanders. However, they tend to address FMS issues in piecemeal at the points where the FMS process intersects with the broader policy system for security cooperation.

One way in which the 2023 FMS Tiger Team's results differ from previous reform efforts is the establishment of the Continuous Process Improvement Board, which is intended to be a permanent accountability structure that tracks progress on recommendations approved by DoD leadership. This report is also a departure from previous efforts in that it scrutinizes the roles, responsibilities, and authorities (RRAs) that undergird FMS-related government organizations in whole, with the understanding that making strides in any of these areas requires effective foundational guidance across and among the FMS enterprise.

Approach

Our research sought to explore challenges across the distinct phases of the FMS process, each with its own set of activities, requirements, and stakeholders with myriad RRAs for

[10] *Select RAND Research on Security Cooperation: 2006–2019*, RAND Corporation, CP-A614-3, 2021.

carrying them out. Thus, our research explored aspects of the following phases of the FMS process: (1) pre–Letter of Request (LOR), which includes the activities necessary to assist the purchaser in defining requirements in sufficient detail to produce a complete LOR; (2) case development, which includes activities that are required to prepare the Letter of Offer and Acceptance (LOA) quality data after an LOR is complete; case development activities are complete when the LOA has been signed by the purchaser; (3) case implementation, when the procurement process for defense articles or services begins; (4) case execution, when contracts are formalized and when delivery, training, and support services are delivered to the partner; and finally, (5) case closure, which occurs in the life of a case when all material has been delivered, services have been performed, other requirements of the LOA have been satisfied, known financial transactions (including collections) have been completed, and the purchaser receives a final statement of account.[11]

Mapping Exercise

The team conducted a mapping exercise to understand which organizations played what roles during which of the phases defined above. To do so, we consulted a wide range of FMS-related legal, policy, and service-level documentation. We relied on these documents to gain a sense of what *should* be occurring and then map it against what *actually* happens in practice throughout the FMS process. This analysis helped to identify RRA pain points that may be impeding the effective and expedient delivery of U.S. defense articles to the partners that purchase them. Chapter 2 and Appendix A provide deeper descriptions of each document that informed our analysis. The mapping exercise also assisted us in determining which organizations to target for interviews. In the end, we conducted 99 comprehensive semistructured interview sessions with 105 government officials in the security assistance community.[12] We specifically chose organizations that held established RRAs within the FMS process, including the Office of the Secretary of Defense (OSD), the Joint Staff, DSCA, implementing agencies (IAs), geographic combatant commands (CCMDs), security cooperation organizations (SCOs), and DoS (Table 1.1). Collectively, these interviews represented a wealth of knowledge and expertise, totaling over 1,300 years of combined experience in the fields of FMS and security cooperation. The depth and breadth of their insights provided us with the confidence that we had captured myriad perspectives across the FMS phases.

Out of the total number of 105 stakeholders we interviewed, 34 percent of interviewees represented DSCA, and 28.6 percent came from the IAs. CCMD interviewees accounted for 17 percent of the total, which included SCO military personnel representing the U.S. Air Force, Army, and Navy. Figure 1.1 illustrates the rates of response to our interview requests and indicates that, percentagewise, DSCA personnel had the highest rate of response to our

[11] For additional information on each phase, see Defense Security Cooperation Agency, *DSCA Manual 5105.38-M: Security Assistance Management Manual*, Department of Defense, 2012.

[12] Some interview sessions included more than one participant.

TABLE 1.1

Stakeholder Interview Tally

Organization Name	Number of Interviewees
DSCA	36
IAs	30
CCMDs	18
OUSD(P)	6
OUSD(A&S)	6
DoS	4
DTSA	3
Joint Staff	2
Total	105

NOTE: In each interview, the team first explained the project and received informed consent, then asked interviewees to describe their background, including years of experience working in FMS-related positions, and current role in the FMS process. We then asked the individual whether they perceived any challenges in the RRAs both in their own organization and in others. Additionally, we asked what other stakeholders had an influence on their own RRAs and if that interaction represented a challenge. We concluded the discussion by asking the interviewee if they had any recommendations on changes to RRAs to improve the FMS process. Some individuals then provided the contact information of others who worked with the FMS process and recommended that we speak with them. DTSA = Defense Technology Security Administration; OUSD(A&S) = Office of the Under Secretary of Defense for Acquisition and Sustainment; OUSD(P) = Office of the Under Secretary of Defense for Policy.

FIGURE 1.1

Interview Response Rates by Stakeholder Group

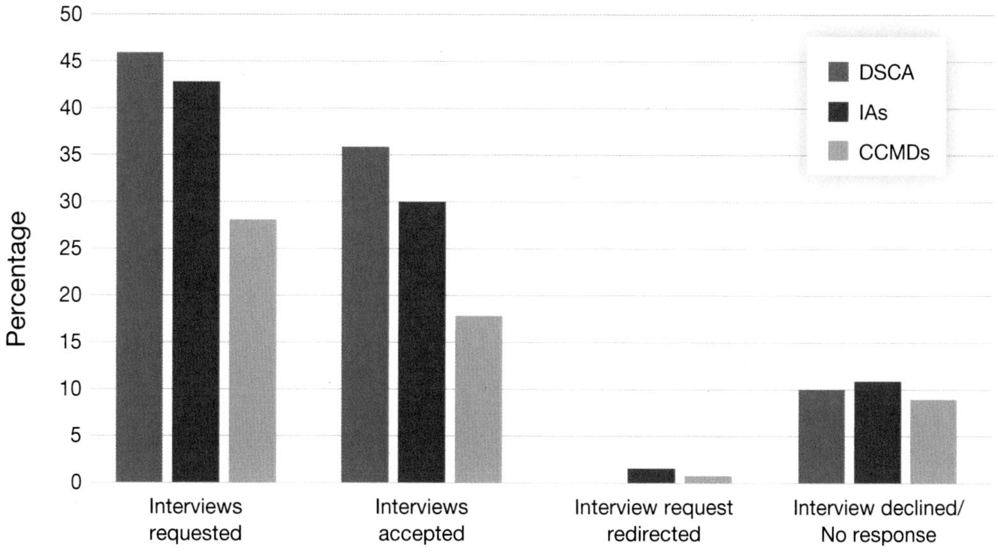

requests for interviews with 78 percent agreeing to an interview, followed by the IAs at 70 percent, and the CCMDs with a 64 percent response rate.

Analytic Shortcomings

While we are confident our analysis covers significant areas of concern for FMS stakeholders, our approach has limitations that are important to note. For one, our research was focused on one dimension of the problem, RRA barriers; we recognize that FMS reform will likely require changes to other inputs to the process (i.e., security cooperation training, human and financial resources, partner purchasing/administrative capacity).

Additionally, quantifying FMS delays proved too difficult to pursue. Early in our research phase, our study team tried to conduct a quantitative analysis of FMS case timelines to corroborate assertions by stakeholders that the FMS case deliveries are stymied by delays, and to understand the nature of those delays. To do so, DSCA provided us with case development data over the past several years (the only phase that the agency can collect on a systematic basis) to help us determine just how long cases remain in this phase and whether there might be relationships between long delays and different types of purchases or partner nations. However, due to the presence of some gaps or inconsistences in the case development data we received from DSCA,[13] we were unable to confidently interpret the results of the quantitative analysis we conducted and to independently quantify the extent of delays in the FMS case development phase. As a result, we relied instead on the qualitative data we collected during interviews.

Additionally, although over half of our interviews were with DoD and DoS organizations, the plurality was with DSCA stakeholders; thus our interview data are skewed toward a DSCA perspective. Engaging with additional stakeholders within the FMS stakeholder community (to include allies and partners) would have undoubtedly shed additional light on ways to further optimize FMS RRAs.

Organization of the Report

In the summary and Chapter 1 of this report, we described RRA challenges affecting the FMS process that emerged during our research and in past reforms. We also described our methodological approach for exploring common themes identified, summarized our recommendations, and offered several caveats that limited our research. In Chapter 2, we enumerate some of the key authorities and guidance documents that guide the FMS program

[13] RAND had difficulty deciphering DSCA's case development data due to what appeared to be inconsistencies in how data are manually entered and a lack of comprehensive information on FMS cases that did not proceed through case development (i.e., cases withdrawn somewhere along the process). It might be possible to conduct a quantifiable assessment of case development timelines with additional time, resources, and access to a data governance guide to better understand the logic behind entries.

before delving into substantive issues regarding insufficient authorities for DSCA. Chapter 3 widens the aperture to examine insufficiencies in how other leading security assistance organizations currently carry out aspects of FMS cases, including DoS, the Under Secretary of Defense for Policy (USD(P)), the Under Secretary of Defense for Acquisition and Sustainment (USD(A&S)), and the Under Secretary of Defense for Research and Engineering (USD(R&E)). Chapter 4 examines operational challenges that the U.S. Air Force, Army, and Navy IAs encounter as they move FMS cases through phases of the process. Chapter 5 digs in deeper into Army-specific challenges with duplicative roles and responsibilities. Chapter 6 concludes the main body of the report with summary thoughts, conclusions, and potential next steps. And finally, Appendix A highlights key authorities and legal frameworks that provided the contours of our mapping of laws, policies, authorities, and other pertinent guidance.

CHAPTER 2

Challenges and Recommendations Pertaining to Defense Security Cooperation Agency Roles, Responsibilities, and Authorities

Overall, the FMS program operates within a comprehensive legal and policy framework designed to ensure that defense articles and services produced by U.S. industry are transferred to foreign partners in a manner that aligns with U.S. and partner national security interests and foreign policy objectives while maintaining appropriate controls and safeguards. This chapter first briefly describes the key documents that govern the FMS process and contain the major RRAs pertaining to DSCA. It then examines the ways in which current RRAs can result in a situation where the agency lacks sufficient authority to carry out its FMS implementation responsibilities. Stakeholders across the enterprise noted these insufficiencies affect the U.S. government's ability to meet the defense needs of important allies and partners fully and expeditiously. The chapter concludes with a set of specific recommendations for amending DoD Directives (DoDDs), specifying the RRAs of DSCA, with the aim of bringing the agency's extensive FMS oversight and management responsibilities in better alignment with its relatively limited enforcement powers.

Authorities in Brief

The FMS process is governed and shaped by a series of laws, policies, and regulations and other guidance documents. We provide a full list in Appendix A but highlight here several key documents that stakeholder organizations rely on to understand and execute their FMS roles and responsibilities. The Arms Export Control Act (AECA), found in Title 22 of the U.S. Code, which outlines the role of foreign relations and intercourse, serves as the foundational legal framework for security assistance, including FMS.[1] It authorizes the President to

[1] In general, the DoS has resourcing and oversight authority over Title 22 security assistance programs, whereas DoD is primarily in charge of security assistance implementation. That said Title 10 of the U.S. Code, which outlines the role of the armed forces, specifies DoD component missions that impact security assistance, such as defense acquisition. Congress has also funded Title 10 security cooperation programs for which DoD have the primary responsibility, some of which are designed to help build foreign

control the export of defense articles and services, including those involved in FMS transactions. The Conventional Arms Transfer Policy (National Security Memorandum 18), which references the AECA and Foreign Assistance Act, as well as the Export Control Reform Act, the NDAA, and the International Emergency Economic Powers Act, also includes roles and responsibilities for FMS and direct commercial sales. In particular, it states that "as decisions regarding arms transfers are important tools for achieving United States foreign policy and national security objectives, the Secretary of State shall coordinate decisions regarding arms transfers with other relevant executive departments and agencies."[2] U.S. Code, Title 10, Section 382, mandates that the director of DSCA "shall be responsible for the execution and administration of all security cooperation programs and activities of the Department of Defense involving the provision of defense articles, military training, and other defense-related services by grant, loan, cash sale, or lease."[3]

DoDD 5132.03, *DoD Policy and Responsibilities Relating to Security Cooperation*, is a directive that outlines the security cooperation policy and responsibilities of various entities within DoD such as OSD, the Joint Staff, the CCMDs, and DSCA. Detailed DoD FMS implementation responsibilities and procedures are outlined in department- and agency-specific directives, instructions, and manuals such as Department of the Army Pamphlet (DA PAM) 12-1, *Security Assistance Procedures and Operations* (2016), which outlines the responsibilities, procedures, and authorities for conducting FMS activities and includes information on case development, pricing, procurement, logistics, and financial management. The Air Force and Navy issue parallel documents to guide their respective forces (i.e., Department of the Air Force Policy Directive 16-1, *Operations Support: Security Cooperation*; Navy International Programs Office Instruction (NIPOI) 4920.3, *Implementation of Foreign Military Sales Case Standard Level of Service Policy Guidance*). DSCA issues the Security Assistance Management Manual (SAMM), which offers a synthesized version of guidance and procedures for administering security assistance programs, including FMS, such as the roles and responsibilities of various stakeholders, acquisition processes, pricing methodologies, and other relevant information. Although the SAMM is an authoritative source for information regarding security cooperation and security assistance, it is not a regulation, directive, or instruction.

Laws, policies, and other documentation exist to direct and guide the actions of leading DoD security assistance organizations responsible for overseeing and managing FMS implementation.[4] However, officials in these organizations assert they lack "line" authority

partner capacity and are colloquially known as "pseudo-FMS" in that they are executed using the FMS process with DoS concurrence.

[2] National Security Memorandum 18, "Memorandum on United States Conventional Arms Transfer Policy," February 23, 2023.

[3] U.S. Code, Title 10, Section 382, Execution and Administration of Programs and Activities.

[4] These organizations include DSCA, OUSD(P), OUSD(A&S), the Office of the Under Secretary of Defense for Research and Engineering (OUSD(R&E)), the Office of the Under Secretary of the Air Force International Affairs (SAF/IA), the Office of the Deputy Assistant Secretary of the Army for Defense Exports and Cooperation (DASA (DE&C)), the Navy International Programs Office (NIPO), and DTSA.

to mandate actions by personnel in subordinate organizations who are tasked with executing relevant policies and directives. As a result, these stakeholders find it difficult to gain visibility into the process and hold organizations accountable for ensuring FMS commitments stay on track. The next section focuses on DSCA's authorities and abilities and highlights numerous areas where DSCA may have insufficient authority relative to its FMS responsibilities.

The Defense Security Cooperation Agency Lacks "Line Authority" over the Organizations That Fulfill Foreign Military Sales Requirements

According to the DoDD that primarily governs its activities, DSCA's overall security cooperation management role is to

- direct, administer, and provide DoD-wide guidance to DoD components and DoD representatives to U.S. missions for the execution of DoD security assistance and security cooperation programs over which it has responsibility (including FMS implementation)
- resource and lead the administration of security cooperation programs for which DSCA has responsibility throughout DoD (including FMS implementation).[5]

Besides having control over the distribution of resources for security cooperation programs, DoD guidance directs that DSCA has several general authorities that it can use to assist in carrying out its managerial responsibilities. The agency can

- communicate directly with the heads of DoD components to ask for their help in overcoming obstacles
- request reports and information to carry out its assigned responsibilities and functions[6]
- develop new security cooperation policies and procedures in coordination with the rest of the security cooperation community and publish them in the SAMM.[7]

The prevailing view we heard from interviewees is that the agency's responsibilities far exceed the authorities needed to ensure that its overarching security cooperation responsibilities are properly executed. From the agency's perspective, law and policy dictate that the director of DSCA is responsible for the administration of all security cooperation programs and activities of DoD involving the provision of defense articles training and other defense-related services by grant, loan, cash sale, or lease, but it has limited control over most of those who directly conduct security cooperation and security assistance activities. As one DSCA stakeholder noted, "No one is responsible for guaranteeing the outcome—nobody knows, nobody can tell you that Chapter 16 of Title 10—I think it says the DSCA should be in charge of this,

---

[5] DoDD 5105.65, *Defense Security Cooperation Agency*, Department of Defense, October 26, 2012, revised March 2, 2013.

[6] While DoD guidance grants DSCA the authority to request reporting information, it fails to identify specific organizations that would be required to provide it. Such ambiguity lends itself to creating loopholes and accountability issues that stakeholder organizations might readily exploit.

[7] DoDD 5105.65, 2013.

but it's not worded strong enough. It [only] says 'You are responsible for . . .'"[8] Another DSCA stakeholder noted, "when things go wrong" and DSCA, and its director specifically, is called to court, "the Secretary of Defense doesn't look at the Secretary of the Air Force [International Affairs] or the DASA DE&C or the Navy IPO [senior leadership], he turns to the DSCA director and asks 'why can't you make this [FMS] system work? You're responsible for it."[9]

For the most part, DSCA stakeholders described relying on "moral suasion" to try to ensure that its policies are executed in a way the agency thinks appropriate. DSCA acknowledges that it does have the "power of the purse" over other DoD components performing security assistance duties—primarily because of responsibility for apportioning funds derived from the administrative fee charged to all FMS customers.[10] But they contend that this resource allocation authority is not a practical tool for inducing behavioral change at the individual or organizational level.[11] Withholding a substantial amount of funding from an FMS IA as an expression of DSCA's dissatisfaction with its performance would likely "just make things worse."[12] Another DSCA stakeholder explained the logic behind this view:

> If [DSCA is] trying to make sure that they're meeting all of the gates on getting something through the LOA process or getting all the technology security things cleared on time, if [it] takes money away from them of course then they'll have less manpower to do that. So, it's not actually going to help them do it better, it's going to make it worse. It's hard to talk about using that as a real forcing function for fundamental things. . . . Having the power of the purse is fool's gold.[13]

Constraints on the agency's ability to more assertively direct FMS cases can result in counterproductive outcomes. For example, stakeholders contend that SCO personnel who lack adequate training can make mistakes that impede the FMS process—for example, not fully or accurately explaining to partner nation representatives the steps and timelines associated with the approval of an FMS request or the delivery of a defense article via the FMS process or failing to regularly engage with defense industry representatives on customer requirements and issues. As the next section describes, DSCA is responsible for managing the security cooperation workforce training, education, and professional development, but it lacks authority to ensure services require that SCO members receive training before taking up their assignments.

---

8 DSCU stakeholder, interview with the authors, March 7, 2023.

9 DSCA official, interview with the authors, May 11, 2023.

10 According to the AECA, DSCA is required to manage FMS at no cost to the U.S. government. The FMS Administrative Surcharge is assessed on the total value of an FMS sale and covers the administrative management costs of the FMS program. Under FMS, the U.S. government uses DoD's acquisition system to procure defense articles and services on behalf of its international partners.

11 OSD official, interview with the authors, May 18, 2023; DSCA official, interview with the authors, May 11, 2023.

12 DSCA official, interview with the authors, May 11, 2023.

13 DSCA official, interview with the authors, March 8, 2023.

The Defense Security Cooperation Agency Lacks (and Is Currently Seeking) Administrative Control over Embassy Security Cooperation Organizations

Security Cooperation Organization Training

By law, DSCA is charged with managing the Security Cooperation Workforce Development Program with the goal being to recruit, train, educate, promote, and retain high-quality security cooperation personnel. This includes ensuring that the workforce possesses skills to develop partner country capabilities in support of U.S. objectives through various DoD- and DoS-funded programs, such as FMS. Only DSCA has authority to issue security cooperation training certifications and permissions for key security cooperation personnel, such as SCO chiefs, to waive required security cooperation training.[14] However, DSCA does not have the authority to compel DoD personnel headed to SCO assignments to attend a training course that teaches the basics of the FMS process and the SCO's role in that process, among other things. Thus, a large but unknown percentage of them do not take the course.[15] One DSCA official described his frustration regarding a situation of an SCO chief who had not attended training and had not received a training waiver, yet there was little the official could do about it. "We have no UCMJ [Uniformed Code of Military Justice] authority. We have no punishment mechanism: I can't stop their pay, and I can't reprimand them. So, what do you do?"[16]

According to DSCA officials, the SCO training deficit has had negative consequences for FMS case development and supporting infrastructure.[17] For example, the SCO plays—or should play—an important role in ensuring the actionability of the LOR, at least when it comes to "novice" partners who are not well versed in the FMS process. Acquisition subject-matter expertise in addition to security cooperation training may be required for actionable LORs for complex FMS cases. However, more than one stakeholder felt that SCO members were sometimes unprepared initially to assume this role. As a result, a great deal of time is spent explaining what is required to move forward with case development. If SCO personnel do not receive adequate training, one IA stakeholder observed, "they're at a great disadvantage and the products that we get to execute are not what they need to be so it can really elongate that process, or you end up with a product that you're just constantly changing."[18]

Yet, DSCA's authority over the training of SCO personnel is just one aspect of the problem. Staff selection is another. As the next section discusses, DSCA is responsible for estab-

---

[14] DoDD 5105.65, 2013.

[15] DSCA official, interview with the authors, March 24, 2023.

[16] DSCA official, interview with the authors, March 15, 2023.

[17] In response, according to feedback received from a SAF/IA official on January 11, 2024, "IAPA [Secretary of the Air Force International Affairs International Airmen Division] supports DSCA's effort to improve SCO training and ensures all SCO personnel receive the full complement of mandatory SCO training prior to their assignments." Also see Air Force IA stakeholder, interview with the authors, June 13, 2023.

[18] DSCA official, interview with the authors, March 28, 2023.

lishing overall qualifications for SCO members, although until recently it has lacked authority to ensure that the CCMDs make appropriate requisitions for SCO personnel and that the services select qualified staff for SCO positions.

Security Cooperation Organization Staff Selection

In coordination with the CCMDs and the services, DSCA is responsible for ensuring the embassy SCO workforce is appropriately sized, selected, and deployed to support security cooperation priorities.[19] Furthermore, DSCA must provide functional oversight of DoD elements in foreign countries responsible for managing security assistance and security cooperation programs.[20] Historically, however, the CCMDs and, to a lesser extent, the services have largely managed the SCO staffing and selection process. Yet, their own interests and views on professional development for their officer and noncommissioned officer corps do not necessarily align with DSCA's imperative of "getting the right people in the right place."[21] In the words of one SAF/IA stakeholder, "The services promote people; the DSCA does not. What you ultimately may do is discourage people from doing those assignments because they realize they're not going to get promoted."[22]

In the same vein, comments from one SCO member from the Air Force we spoke with about manning issues support this point: "Fundamentally in the security cooperation enterprise, it doesn't attract—it's not a desirable place for us to be to enhance our careers. It is mostly a negative on a career so it's difficult."[23] The interviewee continued to describe how the security cooperation workforce struggles to recruit "high performers" because the mission is not viewed as a priority mission among the U.S. military community more broadly: "I will say we're not going to get the services' top performers. The DoD doesn't really care about this enterprise. Or at very least it's a long second. . . . Training equipping our foreign partners is well below everything else. . . . If this were baseball, it's definitely the minor leagues."[24]

This perspective on the quality of SCO personnel was not universally held by members of the security cooperation community with whom we spoke. In particular, IA officials made known the importance placed on ensuring the rigorous selection of individuals filling SCO positions and that those selected for these positions were adequately trained. According to a SAF/IA official, "IAPA, which handles the Air Force's nomination process got very serious in the past few years about the selection of SCOs—the professionalization of that officer role."[25]

---

[19] DoDD 5132.03, 2016.

[20] DoDD 5105.65, 2013.

[21] DSCA official, interview with the authors, February 8, 2023.

[22] Air Force IA stakeholder, interview with the authors, June 13, 2023.

[23] SCO member, interview with the authors, March 14, 2023.

[24] SCO member, interview with the authors, March 14, 2023.

[25] Air Force IA official, interview with the authors, February 22, 2023.

In this vein, according to another SAF/IA stakeholder, the Air Force has developed a robust system to train SCO personnel and separated out the Foreign Area Officers (FAOs) who usually fill SCO billets "into a program run by SAF/IA and managed as a separate career field. We make sure to take care and promote through the FAO career path, rather than having them rely on their other career field."[26]

Nevertheless, the Air Force SCO member's quote above regarding the struggle to recruit high performers to fill out SCO positions was not a singular observation. Another stakeholder we interviewed described how some CCMDs or services have selected soldiers, sailors, or airmen who had no prior understanding of the FMS process. "It could be some guy that was just deployed in Iraq [maintaining missiles] and didn't touch security cooperation."[27] To ensure more strategic and effective staffing, some interviewees from DSCA contend the agency should have a major role when it comes to SCO staffing and selection.[28]

To address the issues associated with the current system of SCO staffing and selection, the SECDEF has recently granted DSCA the authority in the near term to develop, deploy, and administratively control DoD civilian employees[29] who might provide continuity and augment, or in some cases replace, military personnel who rotate more often than civilians do and who might be less qualified in terms of security cooperation experience.[30] In the longer term, once it has increased its managerial capacity, DSCA will acquire additional administrative control over SCO military manpower resources. One DSCA stakeholder asserted that the agency has committed to maintaining "a close dialogue with the CCMDs on their requirements and needs, as well as with the current SDO/DATTs [Senior Defense Official and Defense Attaché] and SCO chiefs." In addition, it will conduct a global survey of SCO manpower "to ensure that we have enough people in the right place based on workload and national security priorities." At that point, it will begin to make workforce adjustments, to include "pulling people from on CCMD to support another."[31]

The Defense Security Cooperation Agency Mostly Delegates the Execution of Foreign Military Sales–Related Activities to Service Implementing Agencies

According to DoDD 5105.65, DSCA and OUSD(P) are responsible for overseeing the implementation of high-priority and urgent FMS cases and related activities to ensure they are

---

[26] Air Force IA stakeholder, interview with the authors, February 14, 2023.

[27] DSCA stakeholder, interview with the authors, March 28, 2023.

[28] DSCA stakeholder, interview with the authors, February 8, 2023.

[29] DoD, 2022.

[30] DSCA stakeholder, interview with the authors, February 9, 2023.

[31] DSCA stakeholder, interview with the authors, February 8, 2023.

executed in a timely and effective manner.[32] However, DSCA delegates the day-to-day administration of most security cooperation programs, including FMS, to the military departments and other DoD components.[33] In most cases, stakeholders we spoke with felt the oversight-executor relationship between DSCA and the service IAs responsible for developing FMS cases works well enough to achieve established goals. But when something goes awry in this complex process, especially with respect to cases involving major allies or strategically important partners with access to senior U.S. government leaders, DSCA officials perceive they are on the hook to find a fix, yet have insufficient authority to uncover the source of the problem if it involves service IA personnel or to hold IA organizations or individuals accountable for fixing the problem.[34] As one interviewee put it, "Our stick is relatively limited on how we can influence change."[35] The interviewee elaborated on this point:

> The real issue [for DSCA] is we don't have tasking authority over the IAs. The DSCA director . . . can put out certain policies in the SAMM or [as] general guidance, [but] we can't tell an IA to do X Y Z. There's a lot of collaboration that occurs at all levels. I work with my counterparts in the IAs. If there's an issue that comes up, I can voice it to them. But I can't tell them to do things. I think the same thing happens at all levels.[36]

One component of the FMS process in which DSCA officials expressed frustration with service IAs is the LOR phase, when IAs and SCOs engage with foreign partners to discuss partner capability gaps and needs and the extent to which they might be addressed through FMS. One DSCA interviewee stated, "There are real challenges in collecting [pre-LOR] information." DSCA must

> ask really nicely to the IAs to get this information [e.g., how many pre-LOR conversations you've had with a partner on these dates] and for them it may not even be documented. . . . It's not a priority to them it's not their boss asking for it. . . . I've never had anyone say no, but silence speaks volumes. Or it's nine months later that I might get something, and there's no way to determine how accurate that something is.[37]

---

[32] DoDD 5105.65, 2013.

[33] DoDD 5105.65, 2013.

[34] One DSCA official indicated that the IAs differ regarding the extent to which they are transparent with DSCA about their FMS implementation challenges. From his standpoint, one IA was "extremely good" about discussing major cases and letting DSCA know "ahead of time if something's going to break," whereas another IA was not very responsive to DSCA's requests for information; the third IA fell somewhere in between the other two on the transparency spectrum. DSCA official, interview with the authors, May 11, 2023.

[35] DSCA official, interview with the authors, March 13, 2023.

[36] DSCA official, interview with the authors, March 13, 2023.

[37] DSCA official, interview with the authors, March 28, 2023.

DSCA-IA friction points also come into sharp relief during the TSFD process.[38] During this process, the IAs shepherd a requested FMS case through potentially multiple U.S. government organizations responsible for approving the transfer of classified information or sensitive technologies for which they are responsible to foreign governments and international organizations. Stakeholders indicated the process can be notoriously slow and opaque, especially in complex FMS cases, such as the F-35 Lightning combat aircraft, which must pass through as many as 13 different review and approval "pipes" with multiple controlling organizations, any one of which can prevent a case development deadline from being met.[39]

Obscurity makes the situation worse. As with the pre-LOR phase, a large part of the TSFD problem for the department concerns a lack of transparency across the process due to stovepiping. As one interviewee explained, "We don't know about [a TSFD issue] until it's too late to do anything about it."[40] For example, if a case is held up in one "pipe" for 18 months and the overall case development metric is 150 days, DSCA is at a loss to explain the nature of the issue to the customer or senior U.S. government officials—much less determine whether the delay was avoidable, even less so estimate the time it might take to obtain the necessary clearance—without open lines of communication with the IAs.[41]

DSCA's ability to oversee those responsible for carrying out this process is indeed rather limited. According to DoD directives, DSCA has two primary roles. The agency

- supports the development of foreign disclosure and sales policies for defense information, technologies, and systems (in coordination with USD(P) and USD(A&S))[42]
- jointly manages with USD(P) the Strategic Planning and Support Group, which was supposed to identify partner capability requirements that may require DoD-level TSFD reviews and mitigation plans based on a recommendation by the 2011 SCRTF.[43]

It is our understanding that the Strategic Planning and Support Group was approved by the 2011 SCRTF. We reviewed the guidance regarding this matter and found that DSCA's authority in this group was approved by SECDEF but never implemented.

As the next section discusses, DSCA's frustrations with its lack of authority over the military departments extends beyond the case development stage of FMS.

[38] We will discuss the important role of DTSA in the TSFD process in Chapter 3.

[39] DSCA official, interview with the authors, March 28, 2023.

[40] DSCA official, interview with the authors, May 11, 2023.

[41] DSCA official, interview with the authors, March 28, 2023.

[42] DoDD 5132.03, 2016.

[43] DoDD 5105.65, 2013; input from DSCA official, December 12, 2023.

The Defense Security Cooperation Agency Lacks Authority to Ensure That Service Contracting and Acquisition Officials Report Progress on Foreign Military Sales Case Execution

According to one OSD official, the agency is "held accountable" when a partner government official elevates an issue with a case to the highest levels of DoD.[44] Within DoD, this issue is typically first directed to the pertinent USD(P) regional desk, which then notifies DSCA. At that point, DSCA "has to go all over the moon, earth, and sun to find out where the case is and what the holdup is."[45] And when the issue involves case execution as opposed to case development, DSCA has few mechanisms to pressure contracting and acquisition officials outside its chain of command, other than appealing for help to senior officials in the military departments or USD(A&S).[46] One interviewee summarized the problem as being that once an LOA is signed with a partner, specifying what the United States will deliver in terms of defense articles and services and how much the partner will pay, the FMS case is "in the hands of the U.S. acquisition system," whose primary mission is to equip U.S. military forces, not foreign forces. Service acquisition officials "have nothing in their directives that tell them that they have a stake in or an interest in or can be held accountable for" helping to build foreign partner capabilities. As a result, DSCA "has been fighting to even get the data" on security assistance acquisition cases.[47] One interviewee reported that DSCA attempted to gain the authority to direct efforts to establish common security assistance data standards and data mining policies. But these efforts floundered when the agency tried to encompass the acquisition dimension of security assistance, which was "still seen as a completely separate entity" from the members of the security cooperation community and hence not subject to DSCA's dictates.[48] According to a DSCA official, the Deputy Secretary of Defense during the Trump administration issued a memo that instructed the services to develop a plan to share FMS execution data, and the services took no action until SECDEF renewed the requirement during the Biden administration at the recommendation of the 2023 FMS Tiger Team.[49]

DSCA's lack of situational awareness in the execution phase is particularly acute with respect to the negotiation, preparation, and application of FMS contracts with U.S. industrial suppliers.[50] Under existing authorities, one interviewee noted, DSCA had "no visibility or knowledge of the contracts between the IAs and the company providing the defense article

[44] OSD official, interview with the authors, May 2, 2023.

[45] OSD official, interview with the authors, May 2, 2023.

[46] DoDD 5105.65, 2013.

[47] DSCA official, interview with the authors, March 23, 2023.

[48] DSCA official, interview with the authors, March 20, 2023.

[49] Input from DSCA official, December 12, 2023.

[50] DSCA official, interview with the authors, March 10, 2023.

or service." For example, DSCA is not notified of a contractual dispute "in the vast majority of cases." If there is litigation, DSCA is only notified when its support is required, usually in the form of money needed to settle a case, which the litigants may hope to obtain from the funds set aside for FMS purchases by the foreign buyer, a situation that could have serious diplomatic repercussions.[51]

The Defense Security Cooperation Agency (Among Other Organizations) Lacks Authority to Access Critical Foreign Military Sales Data Housed in Disparate Locations Across the Foreign Military Sales Enterprise

As previously mentioned, a common theme that emerged during our discussions was that the FMS community lacks a coordinated approach to data governance across the enterprise. The problem is occurring due to the decentralized nature of FMS data management systems, which has resulted in siloed data management practices and a lack of standardization in data collection, storage, and sharing. An IA stakeholder we spoke with described a deluge of competing systems that makes it difficult to divine optimal FMS process decisions: "We've got 47,000 different databases with stuff in it. The phrase that I use is that we are data rich and information poor."[52] A DoD policy-level official similarly described this situation: "All the different services use different systems, and the data doesn't communicate." Although technical fixes to the problem of data aggregation across the security cooperation and security assistance community have been under development for some time, this official claimed that "there's no way to correlate everything together into any kind of easy to digest picture to show where any specific contract is on any specific day."[53] Fortunately, he had been able to establish contacts in the contracting office to facilitate access to information when needed:

> I'd say, "give me a status on this contract or give me a status on this delivery. When's it going to be done?" I would say the vast majority of the time they were able to help but the fact is that we don't have the level of transparency or visibility into the inner workings of the contracting side of the house. That creates anxiety and causes friction. . . . You create motion and movement in that acquisition phase by having a better understanding of where the contracts are.[54]

Our interviews indicate that the highly decentralized system is a trade-off and unintended consequence of pushing data systems down to the service level to enable personnel to

[51] DSCA official, interview with the authors, March 21, 2023.

[52] IA stakeholder, interview with the authors, March 29, 2023.

[53] DoD policy official, interview with the authors, March 21, 2023.

[54] DoD policy official, interview with the authors, March 21, 2023.

have fingertip access to the information required to implement cases in an expedited fashion. As one DoD policy-level official explained,

> It changed in recent years. It's a balance of letting the MILDEPs go fast versus understanding what the data is. . . . We struggle today now at the OSD level to get acquisition data from the services for US programs of record, for DoD programs. But there has not been a desire to go back to heavy oversight.[55]

The impact of this problem is that it affects a wide range of organizations across the government, including DSCA as the lead administrative agency for FMS.

Summary

DSCA encounters authority challenges with respect to embassy SCOs and MILDEPs that limit its ability to oversee and manage the FMS implementation process. In the pre-LOR stage, DSCA struggles to ensure the quality of partner capability requirements and requests because it cannot rely on the security cooperation training and qualifications of SCO personnel who are supposed to assist partners in developing and submitting their LORs. Data inaccessibility makes it difficult for DSCA to ensure the timeliness and quality of IA case development activities, such as TSFD, and maintain situational awareness of MILDEP contracting and production activities in the case execution phase. Ideally, major FMS implementation issues between DSCA and the IAs could be resolved through institutional mechanisms, such as the Strategic Planning Support Group, which is cochaired by OSD-P and DSCA and includes representatives from the IAs and CCMDs. However, as stated earlier, this group has never been stood up, and other high-level coordinating bodies have proved ineffective from DSCA's standpoint. This has led us to recommend certain changes to DSCA's RRAs to help ensure that strategic-level FMS policies are being properly executed by members of the security assistance community and procedural problems can be quickly assessed and addressed before they have serious international consequences.

Defense Security Cooperation Agency Recommendations

As a starting point for providing DSCA the authority necessary to carry out its FMS responsibilities, we recommend that DoD amend key policy directives. DoDDs provide guidance, instructions, policies, and procedures for the entire department. OSD plays a role in drafting, reviewing, and implementing these directives, which SECDEF ultimately issues as legally binding documents that convey DoD's goals, objectives, and expectations to its various components, agencies, and personnel. DoDDs are typically at the highest level of a documen-

[55] DoD policy official, interview with the authors, June 2, 2023.

tary hierarchy that includes instructions, manuals, regulations, and other types of guidance. DoDDs have a binding nature within DoD, meaning that DoD personnel and organizations are obligated to follow them. Failure to comply with DoDDs can result in disciplinary action.[56]

Our recommendations propose documentary revisions that describe DSCA's RRAs as a defense agency (DoDD 5132.03) and in relation to other major stakeholders in carrying out the department's security cooperation mission (DoDD 5105.65). These amendments include giving DSCA (1) administrative control over SCO-bound personnel as well as approving authority for SCO billet descriptions and, *where appropriate*, SCO chief selections;[57] (2) the ability to recommend FMS-related criteria that should be addressed in SCO chief evaluations; (3) a role in the process of selecting top IA leaders and evaluating their performance;[58] (4) the authority to demand regular reports from the MILDEPs on the contracting and production status of FMS cases; and (5) the authority to establish a new security assistance data czar position responsible for overseeing data governance across government agencies, working to establish standardized data management practices and ensure data quality, security, and accessibility.

The data czar would also work to promote collaboration and information sharing across agencies, as well as industry stakeholders and international partners, helping to break down silos and improve overall data management practices. The czar would not be mandated to change the systems themselves, but rather would be able to demand awareness of and access to those systems to serve as a conduit for better data sharing. By establishing a centralized approach to data governance, DSCA would have push-and-pull authority over data to get it

---

[56] Washington Headquarters Services, "Frequently Asked Questions About DoD Issuance," webpage, U.S. Department of Defense, undated.

[57] The range of security cooperation activities and responsibilities varies from location to location. Our recommendation is that DSCA should have approving authority in offices where there is a significant amount of FMS or other security cooperation or security assistance activity where DSCA has primary responsibility for directing. DSCA would need to work with the services and CCMDs to establish a memorandum of agreement on which SCOs would fall under this category. We also note that some SCO chiefs wear a second hat as the resident SDO/DATT. As SDO/DATTs selections fall under the mandate of the Defense Intelligence Agency, we would also consider most, or all, of these positions exempt from requiring DSCA's selection approving authority.

[58] Clearly, MILDEP secretaries have the primary role in the selection of military and civilian personnel within their departments, to include the heads of SAF/IA, DASA (DE&C), and NIPO, stemming from their organizational responsibilities under U.S. Code, Title 10, Section 9014, and DoD personnel management policies, such as DoDD 1403.1, *The Senior Executive Service and Equivalent-Level Positions and Personnel*, October 18, 1982. However, the DSCA director's participation in the hiring process need not contravene the MILDEP secretaries' right to organize their departments; nor would it necessarily require modifying existing DoD personnel policies. As a participant in the process, the DSCA director would not be the hiring official or the deciding official. In the case of Senior Executive Service civilians being considered for SAF/IA and DASA (DE&C) leaders, the DSCA director could be an invited nonservice member of the hiring panel whose recommendations would need to be approved by the Air Force's and the Army's Executive Resource Board. With respect to the position of NIPO director, which is held by an admiral, the Navy could consult with the DSCA director on its choice before public release of the selection decision or assignment notification. The particulars could be clarified via memorandums of agreement between the MILDEPs and DSCA.

from where it is stored to where it needs to be. It is important to note that this does not solve the problem of the defense industry and production capacity challenges that make it difficult to deliver on timelines but would at least solve for lack of visibility into the acquisition and contracting status of cases so they can communicate, troubleshoot, and potentially head off disappointed partners in the process.

Table 2.1 summarizes our recommendations aimed at enhancing DSCA's ability to more effectively fulfill its FMS commitments.

The recommendations outlined above are not intended to diminish the FMS-related RRAs of the CCMDs, IAs, or MILDEP contracting and systems commands. DSCA will remain a

TABLE 2.1

Recommended Changes to Guidance to Increase the Defense Security Cooperation Agency's Foreign Military Sales Authorities

Challenge	Recommendation
Recently approved recommendations to SECDEF to increase DSCA's administrative control over SCOs workforce to improve personnel training, qualifications, and performance do not include modifications to DSCA's RRA in DoDDs.	• Amend DoDD 5132.03 and/or DoDD 5105.65 to state that all personnel selected for SCO assignments shall be transferred to DSCA administrative control for training before taking up their assignments; additionally, DSCA will have approving authority over all SCO billet descriptions and, where appropriate, SCO chief selections. DSCA will also recommend FMS-related criteria that should be addressed in SCO chief evaluations.
DSCA lacks the authority to hold service IA officials accountable for failing to meet case development timelines and standards and to keep it apprised of problems related to major FMS proposals and cases.	• Amend DoDD 5132.03 and/or DoDD 5105.65 to state that the director of DSCA will participate in the process of selecting top leaders at SAF/IA (one Senior Executive Service civilian), DASA (DE&C) (one Senior Executive Service civilian), and NIPO (one U.S. Navy admiral); and will provide periodic evaluations of IAs' FMS case development performance to OUSD(P) and MILDEP leaders.
DSCA lacks the authority to require MILDEP contracting and acquisition officials to provide periodic updates on the status of security assistance–related cases.	• Amend DoDD 5105.65 to state that the MILDEPs have the responsibility for providing accurate and up-to-date information to DSCA, OUSD(P), and OUSD(A&S) on the contracting and production status of security assistance–related cases and any actual or anticipated problems according to standards and procedures approved jointly by OUSD(A&S) and DSCA.
DSCA lacks visibility into key FMS data housed within other FMS stakeholder systems.	• Amend DoDD 5132.03 and/or DoDD 5105.65 to state that DSCA has the authority to establish a data czar with authorized access into all U.S. government data sources pertaining to FMS cases. The role of the czar is to induce MILDEP IAs and acquisition organizations to make security assistance data discoverable by developing clear guidelines, standards, and incentives for data sharing across the enterprise.
DSCA's SAMM is insufficiently authoritative to ensure that DoD components adhere to its security assistance policies and procedures.	• DoD should elevate the SAMM to the level of a DoD Instruction.

primarily policy and managerial organization and must continue to coordinate and collaborate with other FMS stakeholders, and delegate important responsibilities to them, so that the complex components of the FMS enterprise will function properly. Rather, our intention is to enhance DSCA's ability to provide strategic direction with respect to FMS implementation, oversee the development and execution of major FMS cases, ensure alignment with the strategic vision and goals of the individuals chosen for senior leadership positions, and hold other DoD security assistance organizations accountable when they fail to perform as directed. Still, demanding accountability is not enough to improve execution agencies' transparency and performance. And more than one IA stakeholder flagged that inserting DSCA into the selection and performance evaluation processes risked adding a layer of bureaucracy that might slow down rather than speed up FMS deliveries to anxious partners. As one Air Force IA stakeholder warned, "Countries already feel like we are too bureaucratic and worry about whether we can even get the equipment into their hands. They will go to other suppliers because it's just easier."[59]

Other changes will also be needed, such as more, and more highly trained, personnel, as well as compatible information systems and improved analytical tools. The RRAs of other FMS stakeholder organizations might also need to undergo refinement to create more comprehensive improvements to the process. The following chapter explores some of these issues in more detail.

---

[59] Air Force IA stakeholder, interview with the authors, February 14, 2023.

CHAPTER 3

Challenges and Recommendations Pertaining to the Roles, Responsibilities, and Authorities of Other Policy-Level Organizations

DSCA is not the only executive branch organization facing FMS authorities dilemmas. Our research indicates that for myriad reasons, DoS struggles to play an assertive role in FMS policymaking decisions. USD(P) also retains important FMS-relevant authorities to direct their office and subordinate offices. However, USD(P) does not fully or consistently exercise its largely strategy- and policy-oriented FMS roles and responsibilities, in part because of an actual or perceived lack of authority in areas where other organizations have important RRAs. DoD guidance also directs that USD(A&S) and USD(R&E) are responsible for overseeing DoD capability development and acquisition, but these organizations similarly tend to lack "line" authority to ensure that military department officials abide by policies and standards that affect the exportability, contracting, production, and sustainability of defense equipment provided to foreign allies and partners. DTSA's main challenge is that it lacks the authority to ensure that service IAs and review or approving officials from other DoD components follow TSFD policies or meet quality and timeliness standards.

This chapter describes key authorities and discusses how gaps in these authorities play out during aspects of the FMS process.

State's and Defense's Policy Roles Are Sometimes Unclear or Underutilized

The Department of State's Roles, Responsibilities, and Authorities on Paper

Per Title 22, FMS is a DoS program, and the department's roles encompass policy formulation, export control, negotiation and approval of FMS agreements, human rights and regional stability considerations, congressional notification, oversight, and interagency coordination to ensure these sales align with U.S. national interests and foreign policy objectives.[1]

[1] U.S. Code, Title 22, Sections 2751–2776.

The Department of State's Roles, Responsibilities, and Authorities in Practice

While on paper DoS features prominently in the FMS process, our interviews suggest the department's imprimatur has been somewhat muted, with the exception of its involvement in the congressional notification process—though perspectives on why this is the case differ by organization. For example, a DSCA stakeholder noted the lack of strategic guidance from DoS regarding what it wants military partners to do:

> What I envision is some overarching plan for FMS with partners and here's how we get to that. Instead of telling us what a partner should buy, tell us what role the partner should play, and we'll figure out a plan for that. If State gives guidance to Policy, Policy can figure out how the DoD will meet the demand or go back to State to start a dialogue. It would be awesome if State put out some guidance for what we want to do with the partner.[2]

Other stakeholders reminded that as a Title 22 program, DoS has the authority to determine which partners the program should prioritize in accordance with foreign policy objectives. Yet, DoS tends to provide insufficient or ad hoc guidance, leaving DoD to set the stage in terms of which partners to prioritize. As a DSCA stakeholder observed,

> We've worked with them in certain contexts to agree on some priorities, but it's a little bit more informal. Where there is prioritization, lately it's been sort of DoD generated. Or it's really temporal well so and so is going out to the region now the president's going here. . . . It changes by administration. It's pretty ad hoc.[3]

A DoD policy-level official noted,

> It is a DoS-led process. So, the ability for DoD to shape that guidance is—it's an area to work with DoS on. I do think that over all there are Security Assistance functions that DoD takes on behalf of State—obviously DSCA. I would say there's confusion in the process, there's conflicting priorities being given.[4]

While these stakeholders felt DoS had somewhat abdicated its FMS policymaking responsibilities, DoS stakeholders we spoke with held a different view, believing that the problem stems from DoD's reluctance to engage with them on various matters, leaving DoS largely "iced out" and unable to collaborate effectively with DoD in developing policies and addressing issues:

> There is sometimes a refusal to engage the State Department on an issue until a DoD position is blessed by the Secretary of Defense or the deputy Secretary of Defense. That ices us

---

[2] DSCA stakeholder, interview with the authors, June 16, 2023.

[3] DSCA stakeholder, interview with the authors, May 2, 2023.

[4] DoD policy-level official, interview with the authors, March 24, 2023.

> out in terms of cooperation and collaboration and trying to develop policies.... It is really significantly impacting the security cooperation enterprise.[5]

The scope of our research prevented us from arbitrating these views more thoroughly. That said, we felt it instructive that the relationship between the two leading security assistance organizations does seem somewhat distanced as it pertains to FMS issues. As evidence of this, the recent Tiger Team study did not include DoS representation among participants who examined key FMS challenges for the broader enterprise. Furthermore, DoS concurrently conducted its own FMS review initiative titled "FMS 2023: Retooling Foreign Military Sales for an Age of Strategic Competition," aimed at similar concerns with FMS processes and activities.[6] Reportedly, both departments decided to "get their own houses in order" first before engaging with each other on FMS challenges affecting them both.[7] However, it is reasonable to surmise that the departments' independent approaches potentially missed opportunities to establish a unified vision and voice to advocate, facilitate, and possibly accelerate FMS cases through a streamlined approach when issues arise.

Stakeholders also described how DoS's somewhat muted presence within the FMS process creates confusion and potential delays as stakeholders navigate through the fuzzy distinctions between Title 22 and Title 10 authorities.

> Our relationship with some of the other DoD entities is starting to become fuzzy. . . . Within strategy, who does what between them? It's gotten very confusing for us and for our counterparts outside of our agency on who they're supposed to be working with. . . . The roles and responsibilities for a particular country's program has really morphed and we've become stove piped and we're having a hard time differentiating between roles and responsibilities when it comes to FMS versus BPC [building partner capacity].[8]

Other CCMD stakeholders described the time required to deconflict Title 10 and 22 authorities to fulfill their day-to-day requirements. One CCMD stakeholder noted how FMS and BPC funding profiles "could switch day by day. We're looking at getting some type of clarity of this issue through manpower studies, but it's a bit hazy now."[9] Another CCMD stakeholder described spending time deciphering between authorities to ensure staff's job duties were funded under the appropriate statute: "In general it's not—after all this time—entirely clear to me how Title 22 is awarded, and upon what criteria they base [it]." The stakeholder discussed the challenges associated with implementing Section 1090 of the FY21 NDAA, which mandates DoD to conduct security vetting for all international students coming to the United

---

5 DoS stakeholder, interview with the authors, June 22, 2023.

6 Office of the Spokesperson, 2023.

7 Input from DSCA stakeholder, January 11, 2024.

8 DSCA stakeholder, interview with the authors, April 20, 2023.

9 CCMD stakeholder, interview with the authors, March 13, 2023.

States for training using Title 10 resources (specifically through Operation and Maintenance, Army dollars). However, complications arise when Title 10–funded training managers must oversee training programs for countries using FMS dollars. As a result, these managers are required to handle the vetting process, even for Title 22 students, leading to potential resource constraints and operational difficulties.[10]

We were unable to ascertain whether, and if so how, a lack of clarity on the distinction between Title 22 and Title 10 authorities affected FMS deliveries. However, one DoS stakeholder implied the confusion led to administrative burdens and confusion for SCO personnel:

> Well, I'm quite concerned about them. I'm quite positive that they're asked to do so many more things now. . . . What's the Secretary of State responsible for, what's Secretary of Defense responsible for, and under what conditions people in the countries are under chief of mission authority and when they're under combatant command authority. They're screwed. There are just little dumb things are happening all the time. And again, there's a lack of understanding sometimes between what's FMS and what's BPC. They manage these things and conflate them.[11]

There is a risk to efficiency when FMS stakeholders, including SCO personnel, lack a clear understanding of how to distinguish between, much less prioritize among, the multitude of security assistance requirements they might be tasked with, including FMS. DoS could do more to provide strategic guidance to security assistance stakeholders across the enterprise. We offer several recommended areas for improvement pertaining to DoS below.

Department of State Recommendations

Our interviews suggest that DoS plays a largely informal role in how DoD plans and implements FMS cases. We believe DoS should identify opportunities to inform the process more assertively. For instance, DoS's FMS 2023 initiative only goes as far as highlighting how DoS can provide expedited planning assistance to partners already identified as priorities in national security guidance. We propose that DoS, in coordination with DoD, publish clear FMS priorities, consistent with the 2023 Conventional Arms Transfer policy, to guide all FMS case ordering decisions. Example criteria might include a partner's human rights record, political willingness, or legal or policy constraints, among other factors that have implications for whether a potential weapons purchase achieves (or perhaps impedes) U.S. foreign policy objectives. As one DoS official reminded, "It's not just about whether or not a COCOM [combatant command] wants a country to get a piece of equipment or get training. Our role in the process is to evaluate a sale and determine whether or not a sale should take place in the first place."[12] Such criteria undoubtedly already shape decisions regarding which char-

[10] CCMD stakeholder, interview with the authors, February 21, 2023.

[11] DoS official, interview with the authors, July 12, 2023.

[12] DoS official, interview with the authors, June 7, 2023.

acteristics are ideal (and those to avoid) when DoD is considering FMS partners. However, codifying clear red lines and green lights in terms of which countries make suitable FMS partners from a DoS perspective provides objective top-down cover for the difficult process DoD stakeholders must carry out in racking and stacking partner requests.

DoS should also play a more integral role in training and educating staff on the delineation between Title 22 and Title 10 requirements. Providing curriculum injects into DSCU training modules and establishing mobile training teams to participate in security cooperation annual conferences and other convening opportunities are options to consider. Increased opportunities for DoS and DoD security assistance professionals to train together at DSCU or the Foreign Service Institute could also prove beneficial, not only for developing common understanding but also for forging relationships among personnel from key organizations.

We heard more than once that building and maintaining relationships between DoD and DoS stakeholders is critical to facilitating efficient and feasible FMS cases. However, the FMS process requires institutionalized good practices and procedures to ensure that the process continues unabated whether or not positive personal or professional dynamics exist among key stakeholders. These recommendations offer just a few ways to do so.

Challenges Pertaining to the Under Secretary of Defense for Policy's Roles, Responsibilities, and Authorities

The Under Secretary of Defense for Policy's Roles, Responsibilities, and Authorities on Paper

Per DoDD 5111.01, USD(P) is charged with overseeing strategic policy guidance for DoD activities across geographic regions and military functions and domains. This includes overseeing the process for preparing campaign and contingency plans and establishing policy on the conduct of alliances, partnerships, and other defense relationships.[13] USD(P) also oversees the direction and administration of DoD-wide policy guidance for the execution of security assistance and security cooperation programs.[14] Additionally, DoDD 5132.03 directs USD(P) to develop and lead processes to identify and address gaps and adjudicate discrepancies in security cooperation authorities, resources, U.S. military capabilities, and DoD component execution.[15]

The Under Secretary of Defense for Policy in Practice

Despite its overarching defense policy and strategy responsibilities on paper, in practice some stakeholders held the view that USD(P) has not effectively inserted itself into FMS-related

[13] DoDD 5111.01, *Under Secretary of Defense for Policy (USD(P))*, Department of Defense, June 23, 2020.

[14] DSCA, 2012.

[15] DoDD 5132.03, 2016.

policy decisions and struggles to crystallize its role in providing FMS policy guidance, leading to missed opportunities to streamline competing priorities, reduce confusion, and elevate awareness of how FMS supports U.S. foreign policy and military objectives. As one DSCA stakeholder observed, "There is often a sort of confusion about who's taking the lead on a certain thing. It adds a level of staffing and bureaucratic confusion that at times isn't helpful."[16] One IA stakeholder described "competing fiefdoms" within OSD-P, noting,

> Stakeholders in the office see themselves as interlocutors for what [they] want in terms of FMS priorities, but representatives of the regional assistant secretaries and deputy assistant secretaries mostly speak for their offices, not for OSD-P as a whole."[17]

We heard similar concerns at the operational level from the CCMD perspective: "I think that OSD-P is a bunch of well-intentioned dogs, all hooked to the same sled, but running in different directions."[18]

One DSCA stakeholder specifically called out OSD—Global Partnerships (GP) as one of these subordinate offices within OSD-P that has not established a foothold in the FMS ecosystem:

> One thing that GP struggled with is what is their role in security assistance and how do they reflect that knowing that State owns the area? GP [hasn't] been as involved with FMS in the past. They struggle with their authority and how they implement that when it comes to FMS. . . . They don't have a full understanding of FMS and where they fit into it and don't have the bandwidth, so there has been a lot of rewind back to DSCA so we can work together to figure it out.[19]

While some stakeholders asserted that OSD-P has yet to solidify its role within the FMS process, we also heard the opposite view in that OSD-P might be punching above its weight in terms of what it aims to achieve and what it can actually carry out under current authorities. One DoD policy-level official noted that similar to DSCA, OSD-P also has "no enforcement mechanisms. It's mostly persuading and talking to senior leaders in those services to push on their people."[20] A DSCA stakeholder expressed a similar perspective: "[OSD-P] doesn't have a lot of authority but have built themselves up into a mini-State Department. If you ask anyone else in the Pentagon, they'll also say that OSD-P has been pushing past their jurisdiction."[21]

---

[16] DSCA stakeholder, interview with the authors, May 2, 2023.

[17] Navy IA stakeholder, interview with the authors, August 14, 2023.

[18] CCMD stakeholder, interview with the authors, March 2, 2023.

[19] DSCA stakeholder, interview with the authors, June 16, 2023.

[20] DoD policy official, interview with the authors, June 1, 2023.

[21] DSCA stakeholder, interview with the authors, March 3, 2023.

One area where some stakeholders felt USD(P) could play a stronger role is in setting, adjudicating, and communicating in a clearer manner the racking and stacking of worldwide priorities that inform FMS deliveries to foreign partners across all CCMDs, some of which have competing requests.[22] As one stakeholder described, "There are a finite number of resources fought for by an infinite number of players."[23] Given the limited resources various FMS stakeholders fight over, another DoD policy stakeholder stated that USD(P) should be the entity doing FMS case prioritization and adjudication, but "not every case would need to go to that level [the Assistant Secretary of Defense (ASD)]," with the ASD for Strategy, Plans and Capabilities (ASD(SPC)) engaging more in "a racking and stacking."[24] According to another DoD policy stakeholder, the importance of having USD(P) play a stronger role in setting and adjudicating priorities for FMS deliveries across CCMDs lies in the fact that USD(P) has a global perspective that feeds into its ability, on the one hand, to identify and consider second- and third-order effects of the trade-offs involved in the sequencing of FMS deliveries and, on the other hand, "to make the decision about where our strategic interests lie and whether those risks associated with reordering from first-in, first-out are risks that are worth taking."[25]

Although the National Defense Strategy identifies foreign partners that are key to furthering U.S. national security objectives, the broader FMS enterprise currently lacks an overarching entity or organization that is responsible for establishing the criteria for identifying and adjudicating across the entire FMS process who the priority partners are whose FMS deliveries need to be sequenced ahead of other partners who are lower priority. As a result, an FMS delivery can potentially find itself in the cross hairs of competing priorities among a multitude of U.S. government stakeholders whose perspectives on which partners should receive the respective U.S. defense equipment, when, and why can differ dramatically depending on organizational prerogatives.[26] DSCA has historically played a role in the prioritization decisions for FMS deliveries and plans to continue to do so. For example, based on the Tiger Team's recommendation, DSCA has established the Security Cooperation Execution Focus Forum (SCEFF) to forward major FMS case challenges to senior leadership for discussion and resolution. Although the SCEFF does not currently have a prioritization mission, it could potentially be employed as a venue for stakeholders to discuss specific FMS cases that they feel may need to take precedence over others. It is important to note, however, that DSCA has sometimes struggled to expeditiously reconcile divergent views, leading to delays in the process as different organizations stake out and hold fast to their positions. As one DSCA

[22] DoD policy-level official, interview with the authors, March 24, 2023; DoD policy-level official, interview with the authors, May 2, 2023; DoD policy-level official, interview with the authors, June 1, 2023.

[23] DoD policy-level official, interview with the authors, April 21, 2023.

[24] DoD policy-level official, interview with the authors, June 1, 2023.

[25] DoD policy-level official, interview with the authors, May 2, 2023.

[26] DoD policy-level official, interview with the authors, May 2, 2023.

stakeholder explained, "A few years ago, we put together a prioritized list, and several of the combatant commands non-concurred because they didn't agree with who was on the list. It may have taken 18 months to put this together, and priorities changed."[27]

The presence in some cases of competing perspectives on priorities between DSCA and DTSA offers an additional illustrative point. On the one hand, the DSCA director—who reports to USD(P) through ASD(SPC)—has the authority to divert or change the sequence of FMS deliveries to foreign partners from first-in, first-out, and prioritize deliveries for certain FMS cases over others.[28] At the same time, DTSA has authority related to decisions regarding the technologies and information that can be shared with U.S. partners and allies, and how this sharing can take place so that the U.S. warfighter technological and military advantage is preserved.[29] In this vein, DTSA conducts its own risk and partner nation requirement assessments, which might be in tension with DSCA's own assessment of partner nation requirements and delivery priorities. According to a DoD stakeholder, there is at times a disconnect between the priorities that the DTSA director advances and those of the broader DoD FMS community at large, including the USD(P) and the regional ASD.[30] Such misalignments among key DoD FMS stakeholders can have an impact on FMS case timelines, resulting in delays. For example, DoD stakeholders mentioned an instance where DTSA vetoed the release of technology associated with an FMS case based on the agency's independent assessment that the partner nation did not need the respective capability, which was at odds with the SCO's, DSCA's, and the IA's assessment.[31]

Stakeholders tended to assert that preventing cases such as these from lingering in an indecision (or ill-decision) loop requires top-down guidance regarding priorities from DoD leadership. Most stakeholders endorsed USD(P) as the logical focal point for translating DoS security assistance guidance into overarching FMS priorities. Our recommendations address this issue and identify additional potential opportunities to help the office assert its roles and responsibilities to greater effect both for its own bureaucratic needs and to support the facilitation of the FMS process.

Under Secretary of Defense for Policy Recommendations

We propose extending USD(P)'s authority to establish and articulate DoD strategic guidance pertaining to FMS in several ways. With respect to the FMS case prioritization, USD(P)'s ASD(SPC) should provide criteria and guidance that would inform a DSCA-developed prioritization framework for prioritizing FMS cases. This recommendation aligns with the

[27] DSCA stakeholder, interview with the authors, February 9, 2023.

[28] DoDD 5105.65, 2013; DoD policy-level official, interview with the authors, May 2, 2023.

[29] DTSA, "Who We Are: Our Mission," webpage, Office of the Secretary of Defense, undated; DoD policy-level official, interview with the authors, May 2, 2023.

[30] DoD policy-level official, interview with the authors, May 2, 2023.

[31] Navy IA stakeholder, interview with the authors, August 14, 2023.

unimplemented Equipping Prioritization Guidelines recommended by the 2011 SCRTF, which also advocated for prioritization guidance informed by broader strategic objectives related to the partner's role in U.S. foreign policy planning. The FMS case prioritization framework would reflect, support, and align with priority strategic objectives that DoS and USD(P) identify, negotiate, and agree on in advance, with USD(P) having the authority to articulate DoD-wide security assistance objectives, priorities, and implementation guidelines. To bolster this USD(P) responsibility, we recommend amending DoDD 5111.01 and DoDD 5132.03 to state that USD(P)'s authority extends to establishing and articulating DoD objectives, priorities, and implementation guidelines as they pertain to the department's security assistance responsibilities, including FMS.

USD(P) has another role it could play. Our analysis indicates that FMS needs senior-level advocacy and an organization focused on championing its value among a somewhat skeptical warfighter community. The 2022 National Defense Strategy highlights allies and partners as a "center of gravity,"[32] and in at least some cases, U.S. military planners appear to recognize how FMS can contribute to this national security strategy. One DoD policy official described how planners help refine and scope a partner's FMS requirements with an aim to enable the command's interoperability objectives:

> If there's key exercises that we want to accomplish and we know that an ally or partner might need some additional capability associated with being able to execute that, that would then support us in a potential future contingency coalition type of format, those are things that we spend a good bit of time talking with allies and partners about.[33]

Still, the majority of comments in this regard took the opposite position, expressing doubt that U.S. partners would represent a viable alternative to U.S. forces fighting. As one DSCA stakeholder explained,

> What drives the department is contingency planning. That is to only put in a plan those allies and partners we can count on to get there. The organizing construct for the department does not include 90% of partners. The security cooperation guys aren't really part of the plan.[34]

A SCO member held similar views:

> They don't take it seriously. In their defense, they got to have a plan to fight a war that could come out. They want to put their energy into forces that they know they can count on. They don't want to put their energy and time into counting on a foreign force.[35]

---

[32] DoD, 2022, p. 2.

[33] DoD policy-level official, interview with the authors, May 18, 2023.

[34] DSCA official, interview with the authors, March 23, 2023.

[35] SCO member, interview with the authors, March 14, 2023.

Comments from a DoS stakeholder further support this observation:

> That would be another concern that INDOPACOM [U.S. Indo-Pacific Command] would be like, "Oh well, that's not my job. Our focus is our own planning, and someone else is going to worry about security cooperation." It really does have to be imbued with the rest of the combatant commands and the rest of the building. I acknowledge that there's no easy way to do that.[36]

The lack of appreciation for what partners can bring to a combined war fight can have cascading negative effects on the security cooperation workforce in that fewer "high performers" want to work within the field:

> There are such misconceptions out there. . . . The US guys used to disparage the guys supporting FMS saying, "I work for the US you guys work for the Saudis." I spent a lot of time telling everybody that, "no, all these people are working for the United States, but the United States has asked them to go do this job." . . . It's definitely the bottom of the rungs. . . . As far as quality of personnel—they would recruit better if they recruited with a better idea of what we do. Most people don't know what we do. The generals don't understand what we do, so the recruiting for voluntary assignment is poorly understood. I have had several cases of poor performers—some of the most difficult and poor performing people—I've also had a lot of great people too, but we definitely veer towards the lower end of the quality spring.[37]

It is our assessment that OUSD(P) is well positioned to establish connections with and dialogue between security assistance stakeholders and CCMD stakeholders with an aim to articulate how FMS partners and their purchases can assist U.S. forces, or in some cases act in lieu of U.S. forces to achieve mutual security objectives. According to one official, the aim of this kind of initiative is to "buy down risk"—that is, set the conditions in which foreign militaries might participate in or support operations, and thereby become better partners.[38] Our interviews suggest these discussions do take place in an ad hoc fashion. However, we recommend OUSD(P) identify opportunities to integrate export of defense articles (through all means, including FMS and direct commercial sales) into operational planning, bilateral and multilateral training exercises, and other activities to support the warfighter in a more consistent fashion.

The link to accelerating FMS cases in the long run is indirect but nevertheless evident. Raising awareness and elevating the importance of FMS partners to achieving U.S. military objectives can prevent cases from lingering due to competing priorities and also help to attract the best and brightest to the mission, ultimately paying dividends in terms of ensuring

[36] DoS official, interview with the authors, July 21, 2023.

[37] SCO member, interview with the authors, March 14, 2023.

[38] Input from DSCA official, December 12, 2023.

personnel with FMS roles and responsibilities are capable custodians, incentivized to effectively work cases to ensure on-time delivery.

Foreign Military Sales Acquisition Stakeholders

Acquisition on Paper

Following the breakup of the Office of the Under Secretary of Defense for Acquisition, Technology, and Logistics (USD AT&L) in 2018, Congress created two organizations—USD(A&S) and USD(R&E)—to handle most of USD AT&L's policy and oversight functions, while devolving much of the responsibility for managing defense acquisition projects to the military departments.[39] According to the current DoD guidance, USD(A&S) has overall responsibility for supervising the performance of the DoD acquisition system.[40] This includes establishing procurement policies to enable secure, efficient, and effective acquisition and directing the secretaries of military departments and DoD and OSD components in the exercise of acquisition and sustainment functions.[41] USD(A&S) is also responsible for leading the DoD acquisition and sustainment data management effort and for providing capabilities to enable DoD's reporting and data analysis, resulting in timely access to accurate, authoritative, and reliable data.[42] That said, USD(A&S) has only limited defense contracting responsibilities, serving as head of contracting activity for components and activities that do not fall under the authority of a military department.[43]

In large part, USD(A&S)'s RRAs for FMS implementation are not stated explicitly; rather, they are implied by its overall defense acquisition RRA and the dependence of the FMS process on DoD's U.S. defense acquisition system for the majority of its case execution functions.[44] Nevertheless, the 2016 defense directive details several jointly conducted, FMS-related responsibilities for the now-defunct USD AT&L, which logically should fall inside USD(A&S)'s bailiwick once that directive has been updated. These include the following:

- leading the development of policies and procedures for the transfer of defense-related articles, services, and technologies to foreign countries (in coordination with USD(P))[45]

[39] Terri Moon Cronk, "DoD Restructures Its Acquisition, Technology, Logistics Organization," DoD News, March 29, 2018.

[40] DoDD 5135.02, *Under Secretary of Defense for Acquisition and Sustainment*, Department of Defense, July 15, 2020.

[41] DoDD 5135.02, 2020.

[42] DoDD 5135.02, 2020.

[43] DoDD 5135.02, 2020.

[44] DSCA official, interview with the authors, February 17, 2023.

[45] DoDD 5132.03, 2016.

- identifying, prioritizing, and pursuing defense acquisition–related agreements required to facilitate the acquisition and transfer of defense-related articles, services, and technologies to allied and partner nations (in coordination with the USD(P) and DoS[46]
- cochairing the Arms Transfer and Technology Release Senior Steering Group (ATTR SSG) to ensure arms transfer policies and procedures comply with national laws and regulations, including technology security and foreign disclosure requirements (along with USD(P)[47]

Since USD AT&L's breakup, it is not entirely clear in policy nor practice whether USD(A&S) or USD(R&E) has oversight over the MILDEPs when it comes to exportability. However, implicit in the guidance outlined above is that one area of possible FMS-related responsibility that USD(R&E) may share with USD(A&S) is providing DoD-level policy and oversight with respect to embedding exportability to allies and foreign partners into the capability development processes of the military departments.

Acquisition in Practice

The combination of less-than-explicit security assistance responsibilities and a devolution of acquisition authority to the services has contributed to what some stakeholders perceive to be a laissez-faire attitude on the part of USD(A&S) on crucial issues affecting FMS implementation. As one IA interviewee put it, the "very broad sense of lack of ownership" for FMS has led USD(A&S) to refrain from expressing strategic-level "preferences for how things should unfold at the Service level."[48]

DSCA stakeholders we spoke with viewed this deference as one of the primary obstacles to efficient information management, contracting, sustainability, and exportability. In the words of one DSCA interviewee, USD(A&S) and its OSD predecessor USD AT&L "have really been dropping the ball for twenty years" when it comes to working with the services and DSCA on developing a DoD-wide acquisition information management platform that was compatible with security assistance data systems.[49] Instead of telling the services "what to use next" when USD AT&L decided to sunset the previous acquisition information technology system in 2013, "they told the Services to use whatever they want." The result was "even more variance" with respect to data systems integral to security assistance, as well

[46] DoDD 5132.03, 2016.

[47] Although one DSCA official described the ATTR SSG as currently moribund, one of the steering group's specified functions is to serve as a DoD appeals board and mediation body for most TSFD processes when TSFD stakeholders are unable to achieve consensus on proposed release decisions. Input from DSCA official, December 12, 2023. For additional information see: DODD 5111.21, *Arms Transfer and Technology Release Senior Steering Group and Technology Security and Foreign Disclosure Office*, Department of Defense, October 14, 2014.

[48] Navy IA stakeholder, interview with the authors, August 14, 2023.

[49] DSCA official, interview with the authors, March 20, 2023.

as an informational void between FMS case management and execution. And USD(A&S)'s usual response to DSCA when it requests assistance in obtaining security assistance–related acquisition data is "to work with the IAs" (i.e., SAF/IA, DASA (DE&C), and NIPO). According to USD(A&S) officials, there were "decisions made years ago to push reporting requirements to the Services."[50] As a result, USD(A&S) "just gets snapshots of the contracts and relies on [the MILDEPs] to execute their programs." In their view, it is the role of the MILDEP international programs offices to tap into service-specific databases to extract programmatic information to which USD(A&S) does not have direct access. From one DSCA official's perspective, this response is an indication that USD(A&S) has "abdicated their [information management] role."[51]

Without any contracting authority of its own or assistance from USD(A&S), DSCA and other organizations with "a need to know" are left to navigate a system they do not fully understand and try to identify potentially multiple contracting nodes that may be associated with a single problematic FMS case, as one DSCA stakeholder explained: "It's run through [USD]A&S and because of that, we don't have the ability to affect it."[52]

It is important to note that, similar to other lead organizations we have described so far, USD(A&S) has its own challenges with a lack of line authority over its community. For example, like other leading organizations that struggle to overcome transparency issues, USD(A&S) is also subject to a defense contracting system that is "micro-federated" or dispersed across the services.[53] An interviewee noted hundreds, if not thousands, of contracting nodes across DoD, mostly working for military department commands and program offices, albeit none working directly for the security assistance community.[54] Furthermore, each of these contracting nodes "has its own systems . . . its own processes [and its own] priorities," which mostly do not pertain to security assistance cases.[55] One acquisition-focused stakeholder we spoke with further described the challenge: "All the different services use different systems, and the data doesn't communicate. There's no way to correlate everything together into any kind of easy to digest picture to show where any specific contract is on any specific day."[56]

That said, USD(A&S) asserts that the processes used by the DoD acquisition contracting community fulfill reporting requirements spelled out in federal acquisition regulations

[50] DoD acquisition officials, interview with the authors, November 21, 2023.

[51] DSCA official, interview with the authors, March 2, 2023.

[52] DSCA official, interview with the authors, March 1, 2023.

[53] DSCA official, interview with the authors, March 2, 2023.

[54] DSCA official, interview with the authors, February 17, 2023.

[55] DSCA official, interview with the authors, February 17, 2023.

[56] DoD policy official, interview with the authors, March 14, 2023.

and mandated by the Office of Management and Budget.[57] USD(A&S) officials acknowledge, however, that the contracting data being reported may not be sufficiently "granular" to meet the needs of DoD acquisition stakeholders for scheduling information in particular, and few DoD agencies use the information management system that supports the acquisition contracting data repository.[58] Yet "doing something different" in terms of reporting requirements and procedures to meet the needs of FMS stakeholders alone would be challenging given the intertwined nature of domestic and security assistance acquisition and the fact that FMS cases are a relatively small portion of total acquisition contracts.[59]

The acquisition and contracting communities also express frustration with what they view as USD(A&S)'s lack of ability or willingness to apply pressure on the services and U.S. industry suppliers to resolve FMS issues related to contracting. One DoD policy-level official noted that the acquisition community struggles to maintain resources to fulfill both U.S. and FMS acquisition requirements.[60]

> There's a bandwidth challenge too. The acquisition workforce that's supporting the MILDEP requirements and the Security Assistance requirements are often the same. If you just look at the FMS sales numbers, they have continued to increase. I don't think there's been any increases in the contracting workforce supporting that.[61]

The prioritization of domestic deliveries over FMS ones also has an impact on the sequencing in which contract work is prioritized by the DoD contracting workforce, resulting in delays in the processing of FMS cases. This prioritization bias is understandable given that the MILDEPs, within which the acquisition community is largely embedded, are not assigned an international engagement mission in DoDDs. The main purpose of the MILDEPs is to man, train, and equip U.S. military forces; they do not have a similar responsibility to build and sustain U.S. allies and partners.[62] According to one of Navy IA stakeholder we interviewed, "FMS is small compared to the domestic side. And they're understaffed; they got

---

[57] DoD acquisition official, interview with the authors, November 21, 2023; Defense Federal Acquisition Regulation Supplement PGI 204.6, *Contracting Reporting*, effective date February 15, 2024; Defense Federal Acquisition Regulation Supplement PGI 225.73, *Acquisition for Foreign Military Sales*, effective date February 15, 2024.

[58] DoD acquisition official, interview with the authors, November 21, 2023; Federal Acquisition Regulation, UCF 15.204-2, Part I—The Schedule, effective date February 23, 2024.

[59] DoD acquisition official, interview with the authors, November 21, 2023. See also Gregory Sanders, Nicholas Velazquez, Emily Hardesty, and Audrey Aldisert, "Defense Acquisition Trends 2023: A Preliminary Look," Center for Strategic and International Studies, December 7, 2023.

[60] Per U.S. Code, Title 10, Section 1705, the Department of Defense Acquisition Workforce Development Account provides funding for the recruitment, training, and retention of DoD acquisition personnel.

[61] DoD policy official, interview with the authors, June 2, 2023.

[62] See DoDD 5100.01, *Functions of the Department of Defense and Its Major Components*, Department of Defense, December 21, 2010, incorporating change 1, September 17, 2020.

a ton of work to do, and their priority is the . . . domestic contract work. So, they will get to it when they are able to get to it. They do their best but that's not their main priority."[63]

One acquisition stakeholder further described how defense industry subcontractors can have an outsize impact on the contracting process that serves to further slow the FMS process:

> As far as being transparent with the industry partner, it's the contracting process. . . . The problem that this particular industry partner is having was all the subcontractors were not being transparent with detailed invoices or detailed breakdowns of what everything costs. And the reason is because all of the subs don't want to share proprietary information with the prime contractor. So even the [prime doesn't] know why a certain widget costs 50,000 dollars extra. They can't get that information from the subs. At least that's what they explained to us what the problem was.[64]

As a result of these challenges, stakeholder organizations outside the contracting sphere, including USD(A&S), generally obtain little information on the status of an FMS case once it enters the contracting phase until the money for the case is obligated.

Exportability is another issue. Within DoD, the primary responsibility for ensuring that U.S. systems are designed and built with exportability in mind would seem to belong to USD(A&S). According to DoD's major acquisition instruction, MILDEP program managers are responsible for integrating "international acquisition and exportability planning into the program's acquisition strategy beginning at the entry milestone and continuing through all phases of the acquisition process."[65] And this includes conducting an exportability roadmap study relatively early in the capability development process for systems with export potential. USD(A&S) reviews each step of the acquisition process for all systems that have not completed the testing phase, to include each program's exportability plan.[66] For its part, USD(R&E) oversees the "anti-tamper" process within DoD, whereby warrant holders determine the extent of advanced technology protection required for different systems or levels of capability.

That said, it was not always clear to some security assistance stakeholders how the exportability portfolio was apportioned within OSD or, more importantly, whether designing weapon systems so they could be sold and employed by partner militaries was actually a DoD priority.[67] One interviewee asserted that the lack of emphasis on exportability has had serious time and money implications for FMS managers and customers. The interviewee mentioned one case where computer programs for a major equipment sale had to be reconfigured because system designers had not taken exportability into account, which added 18 months to the production schedule and cost at least $40 million. In his words, "somebody needs

[63] Navy IA stakeholder, interview with the authors, April 26, 2023.

[64] DSCA official, interview with the authors, March 13, 2023.

[65] Department of Defense Instruction 5000.85, *Major Capability Acquisition*, Department of Defense, August 6, 2020, revised November 4, 2021, pp. 32–33.

[66] DoD acquisition official, interview with the authors, November 21, 2023.

[67] Navy IA stakeholder, interview with the authors, August 14, 2023.

to take charge" of the exportability component of the capability development process and demand that the services pay more attention to this important security assistance issue.[68]

The issue is more complicated than that, however, as the defense industry has a significant say and may not see it in its interest to build in exportability. As one DoD policy-level official explained,

> Building exportability into a program or a capability or a system costs money. Our industry partners, while they respond great and they do the best they can, that's a cost that has to be taken into account early on. If you don't know that you're going to sell something or if you can't be confident that you're going to sell something or export it to somebody else, then you're not going to spend that extra money to bake that in. I think it makes good sense from a business case analysis because you have that ready to go when somebody does ask for it. But at the same time there's certain levels of risk that I don't have to maintain because I don't report to shareholders.[69]

On the DoD side, the MILDEPs are required to plan for exportability, but they too face the challenges of having to (1) "guess what capabilities we will be selling to each country ten years in the future," (2) secure funding for exportability features early in the capability development process when foreign partners may not have requested the capability, much less committed to purchase it, and (3) be confident that TSFD authorities will approve the transfer of the system to a foreign partner once it has been formally requested. Moreover, DoD lacks a process for prioritizing the allocation of departmental funds to pay for early-stage exportability initiatives.[70] As one Navy stakeholder noted,

> The cost of implementing exportability in a system is almost always borne by the FMS partner(s) late in the system's life when it is most expensive to achieve. The late arrival of funding also inhibits pro-active/anticipatory technology release decisions for the MILDEPs [and other TSFD stakeholders] that are necessary in order to offer an LOA and secure that funding.[71]

Also, because the overall acquisition process is tailored to address the needs of domestic services, challenges with fitting the FMS cases of foreign partners into the overall contracting process translate into potential delays. According to one of the DoD subject-matter experts we interviewed, "It's a 'square peg—round hole' situation. You have this work that is important work. It's being funded by the foreign customer, but we're trying to fit it into the operations of the domestic military departments."[72]

---

[68] Navy IA stakeholder, interview with the authors, August 14, 2023.

[69] DoD policy-level official, interview with the authors, March 14, 2024.

[70] DoD acquisition official, interview with the authors, November 21, 2023.

[71] Input from Navy IA stakeholder, January 22, 2024.

[72] Navy IA stakeholder, interview with the authors, April 26, 2023.

Under Secretary of Defense for Acquisition and Sustainment Recommendations

To increase the chance for accurate, timely reporting of FMS case execution activities, we propose that DoDD 5135.02 be amended to state that USD(A&S) has the responsibility and authority to develop DoD standards and procedures for reporting information on the status and scheduling of acquisition contracting and production, to include FMS cases, and to ensure that this information is readily accessible to DoD acquisition stakeholders such as DSCA. Furthermore, we recommend that USD(A&S) be given the authority to periodically evaluate MILDEP acquisition reporting for accuracy and timeliness.

We also recommend that DoDD 5137.02, DoDD 5135.02, and DoDD 5132.03 be amended to state that USD(R&E) and USD(A&S) have the authority and responsibility to ensure that exportability requirements are clearly defined, documented, and resourced by the MILDEPs early in the acquisition life cycle. Although the resourcing aspect of this recommendation may require legislative approval, it accords with proposed congressional legislation requiring DoD to integrate planning for exportability features into guidance for future defense acquisition programs.[73]

The Defense Technology Security Administration's Challenges Pertaining to Foreign Military Sales Roles, Responsibilities, and Authorities

As previous descriptions in this chapter of the RRAs of leading DoD security assistance organizations demonstrate, an important common role for all of them is ensuring that foreign partner requests for the transfer of defense articles and services are aligned with U.S. government laws and policies regarding technology security and foreign disclosure or TSFD. Although no organization is in charge of the entire TSFD process, DTSA is the preeminent TSFD advisory and policymaking organization within DoD. But much like other leading security assistance organizations, DTSA's enforcement powers are limited.

The Defense Technology Security Administration on Paper

DTSA is responsible for establishing TSFD policies and assisting other organizations to navigate the TSFD process and make technology security decisions, but it lacks authority to ensure that service IAs and reviewing and approving officials from other DoD components follow TSFD policies or meet quality and timeliness standards. According to the DoDD that governs its activities, one of DTSA's main roles is to identify and mitigate national security

[73] See U.S. House of Representatives, *National Defense Authorization Act for Fiscal Year 2024, Conference Report*, December 6, 2023, Section 810, "Updated Guidance on Planning for Exportability Features for Future Programs."

risks associated with the international transfer of advanced technology and critical information.[74] To accomplish this mission, DTSA

- advises SECDEF and the Deputy Secretary of Defense, through USD(P), on DoD technology security efforts and policy matters related to the international transfer of sensitive technology
- develops DoD technology security policies related to foreign transfers of defense-related articles, services, and technologies
- provides a single entry point for priority TSFD reviews and other potential high-visibility TSFD cases
- administers the interagency National Disclosure Policy Committee and supports the activities of the DoD components and other federal agencies to monitor and control the flow of sensitive, defense-related technology, goods, technical data, services, and munitions.

According to DoDD 5105.72, DTSA's designation as a focal point for TSFD is limited to coordination of DoS and Department of Commerce export licensing reviews and management of the National Disclosure Policy system.[75] DTSA does not currently manage other components of the TSFD process—for example, defense system and subsystem exportability, MILDEP technology release policy, the communications security or cryptographic information assurance process, foreign involvement in DoD special access programs, or trade security controls for low observable/counter low observable technologies.

The Defense Technology Security Administration in Practice

Our stakeholder interviews suggest that the RRAs described above accurately reflect the purview and constraints under which DTSA operates. For example, one DSCA interviewee described DTSA's role in the TSFD process as more that of a coordinator and facilitator—a job it increasingly shares with DSCA's weapons division—than a top-down manager.

> They are the interlocutor. People go to them to get the right people together. They have an interesting mission where they can reach down to help unstick things. There is a licensing role as well. They are the wrangler to make sure things are moving on track.[76]

[74] DoDD 5105.72, *Defense Technology Security Administration*, Department of Defense, April 26, 2016.

[75] National Disclosure Policy 1 establishes the framework in which foreign disclosure decisions are made by establishing specific disclosure criteria and limitations, definitions of terms, release arrangements, and other guidance required by U.S. departments and agencies for the release of classified U.S. military information to foreign governments and international organizations. DSCA, 2012.

[76] DSCA official, interview with the authors, March 1, 2023.

DTSA can also elevate important TSFD issues to senior DoD leaders. This interviewee observed, "DTSA has a giant mission and not very many people, so tracking across the board is difficult for them," although they have a large division of engineers that "can get into the nitty gritty [of TSFD problems] to explain things and find solutions." Much like DSCA, DTSA has a lot of responsibility, and even the ability, to fix problems in its domain, but it lacks authority over the services and other agencies to monitor the full gamut of its domain, identify what needs to be done, and ensure its preferred remedies are implemented.[77]

Such an increase in DTSA's authority may not be necessary or desirable. One IA interviewee asserted that DoD is not making full use of existing coordination and collaborative mechanisms to deal with TSFD challenges, noting that the ATTR SSG has been moribund for some time. As a result, DoD leaders are no longer having interdepartmental discussions of major issues related to arms transfer and technology release, at least ones to which the IAs are privy. "If we want to share a capability, to what level of capability are we going to share? We have to have the discussion if we're going to share higher end weapons. So, let's get in a room and have that discussion at the right classification level."[78]

DTSA would have a major role in convening and managing this discussion. But this interviewee was leery of giving DTSA more authority to "second guess [military] departmental policy decisions" regarding the types of partners that should be receiving particular capabilities. The interviewee asserted that DTSA officials, primarily with technical backgrounds have begun to do this more often in recent years in a way that is outside of the "normal TSFD pipes," and that can be "very hard to find redress."

"They're diving into the guts of a proposed case that we've already worked and already obtained all of what we know to be the known authorities necessary to be able to offer a system. Then a DTSA engineer says, 'no the country doesn't need that weapon.'"[79] In this stakeholder's view, DTSA should not have an "outright veto" of LOAs based on its own internal review process.

Furthermore, some of the TSFD "pipes" that service IAs need to navigate in pursuit of release and disclosure approvals are outside DTSA's area of responsibility, and the agency "doesn't have the ability to reach into those processes to help out."[80] That said, the Deputy Secretary of Defense has made clear that DoD needs to establish TSFD timelines and inject

[77] DSCA official, interview with the authors, March 1, 2023.

[78] Navy IA stakeholder, interview with the authors, August 14, 2023. It is important to note that senior-level DTSA officials had an opportunity to review a predecisional draft of this report and refuted this interviewee's perspective, asserting that DTSA acts within the bounds of its technology security remit, and has no decision authority to block FMS sales. Adjudicating these views was beyond the scope of this study.

[79] Navy IA stakeholder, interview with the authors, August 14, 2023.

[80] DSCA official, interview with the authors, March 1, 2023.

"some accountability into the process" to better ensure when release and disclosure requests go into the "pipes" and when the results of these requests come out.[81] However, based on current DoD policies, stakeholders were skeptical that the leading TSFD organization will have the authority to bring about the Deputy Secretary's desired outcome; as a result, stakeholders must largely rely on relationships: "We work with all these same members for years. It's building friendships and relationships. And it's like, if you hold this up when you have a request then they'll hold yours up. Our enforcement mechanism is the no vote."[82]

At a more operational or implementation level, exportability challenges look somewhat different. Implementers are under the gun to implement cases and view cumbersome bureaucratic and security constraints as a major impediment to accelerating the FMS process to achieve strategic objectives:

> The Russians and the Chinese don't have the regulatory restrictions like we do. If we're going to play in this game, we got to be allowed to play fairly with our competitors. Start with the tech security and foreign disclosure. That's cumbersome and slow and I know why we do it: that's protecting our crown jewels. But the bottom line is they're so bureaucratic. By the time we go through those TSFD pipes, the train's left the station. They're so slow because our regulations tell us we have to follow certain procedures in those documents.[83]

Defense Technology Security Administration Recommendations

Although DTSA is the recognized knowledge authority on TSFD policies and procedures—as well as the principal coordinator for resolving major TSFD issues—the agency lacks the authority to ensure that service IAs and other TSFD stakeholders reach timely decisions regarding the release of sensitive technologies and information to prospective foreign buyers of U.S. defense articles and services. Furthermore, even if the ATTR SSG were active, it is a consultative body with no authority to override any TSFD stakeholder on a matter under their cognizance. This argues for a greater concentration of TSFD decisionmaking authority in the hands of DTSA, the ATTR SSG, or both. All said, given the complexity of the TSFD process and the number of interests at stake, such a recommendation is probably premature without further consideration of the scope of proposed authorities changes, as well as their costs and benefits. Accordingly, we recommend that USD(P) and USD(A&S) jointly direct research on the trade-offs of establishing a single authority, building on DTSA and the ATTR SSG, for adjudicating and enforcing decisions throughout (or in certain parts of) the TSFD process.

---

[81] DSCA official, interview with the authors, May 11, 2023.

[82] DTSA stakeholder, interview with the authors, May 9, 2023.

[83] Army IA stakeholder, interview with the authors, May 23, 2023.

Summary

This chapter has discussed a variety of ways in which leading security assistance organizations sometimes struggle to exert their authorities over the FMS process. DoS is somewhat absent from key conversations and decision points regarding FMS strategies, priorities, and the appropriate use of statutory authorities. This leads to confusion among operational and frontline personnel responsible for FMS implementation. Stakeholders largely felt that USD(P) has untapped potential that, if leveraged, could help guide prioritization guidance and advocate in ways that may elevate and thereby expedite the FMS footprint to achieve both partner and U.S. security objectives. For USD(A&S), the primary challenge is ensuring that the MILDEPs pay sufficient attention to security assistance cases when it comes to exportability, contracting, production, sustainability, and the overall industrial base. While DTSA is responsible for establishing TSFD policies and assisting other organizations to navigate the TSFD process, it acts more as a coordinator and facilitator than a top-down manager. Its lack of authority over the services and other agencies to monitor the full gamut of its domain, identify what needs to be done, and ensure its preferred remedies are implemented is a major obstacle to its mission.

Recommendations for Leading Department of Defense Foreign Military Sales Implementation Organizations

To help cope with these challenges, we recommend several amendments to DoS policies, DoDD, and associated activities. Table 3.1 summarizes our recommendations for these leading stakeholder organizations.

In this chapter, we have focused on a fundamental aspect of this systemic problem: the imbalance in FMS-related RRAs accorded to leading policy organizations. To some extent, this inhibits them from enforcing their policies, standards, and timelines on FMS execution. In addition to analyzing the causes and repercussions of these authorities challenges, we have recommended specific changes to DoDD that provide a potential starting point for achieving a better balance between leading organizations' responsibilities and authorities in the FMS arena and thereby making the FMS system more responsive to urgent, high-priority U.S. and partner requirements.

Addressing top-down challenges is not enough, however. A consistent theme we heard from IAs is that their organizations are responsible for overseeing FMS implementation in their domains but lack authority to ensure that service IAs and acquisition officials outside their chains of command develop and execute FMS cases according to their policies and standards. In the next chapter we explore this issue in more detail to understand whether these challenges might stem from gaps in existing authorities, lapses in actual execution, or both.

TABLE 3.1

Recommended Changes to Guidance to Increase the Authority of Leading Department of Defense Foreign Military Sales Implementation Organizations

Challenge	Recommendation
Title 22 gives DoS authority to establish FMS strategic guidance and set priorities for FMS cases, yet DoS is sometimes absent from critical FMS decision points.	• DoS should develop and articulate clear department partner prioritization criteria that align with foreign policy objectives.
Lack of clarity on Title 22 and Title 10 roles and responsibilities can create delays.	• DoS should contribute to FMS-related training and education events to clarify Title 22 authorities and associated roles and responsibilities.
OSD-P struggles to crystallize its FMS responsibilities, leading to missed opportunities to streamline competing priorities, reduce confusion, and elevate awareness of how FMS supports U.S. foreign policy and military objectives.	• ASD(SPC) should inform a DSCA-developed standardized FMS prioritization decision tool that incorporates and builds on DoS guidance regarding the partner's role in U.S. strategic planning based on objective criteria. • OSD-P should require regional desks to attend the SCEFF prioritization process to increase interagency collaboration. • OSD-P should encourage CCMDs to integrate partners' FMS-acquired capabilities into operational planning, combined exercise programs, and other opportunities to support the warfighter combined exercise program. • Amend DoDD 5111.01 and/or DoDD 5132.03 to state that OSD-P's authority to establish DoD strategic guidance with respective to foreign partners and allies, to include addressing capability gaps, extends to FMS as well as other security cooperation programs.
USD(A&S) lacks responsibility and authority to ensure that MILDEP acquisition officials provide regular and accurate information on the status and scheduling of acquisition contracting and production, including for FMS cases.	• Amend DoDD 5135.02 to state that USD(A&S) has the responsibility and authority to develop DoD standards and procedures for reporting information on the status and scheduling of acquisition contracting and production, to ensure this information is readily accessible to DoD acquisition stakeholders, and to conduct periodic evaluations of MILDEP acquisition reporting for accuracy and timeliness.
USD(R&E) and USD(A&S) lack authority to ensure that exportability is embedded in the MILDEP capability development processes.	• Amend DoDD 5137.02, DoDD 5135.02, and/or DoDD 5132.03 to state that USD(R&E) and USD(A&S) have the authority to ensure that exportability requirements are clearly defined, documented, and resourced by the MILDEPs early in the acquisition lifecycle.
DTSA and the ATTR SSG lack authority to make and enforce TSFD decisions related to proposed security assistance cases.	• USD(P) and USD(A&S) should jointly direct research on the trade-offs of establishing a single authority for adjudicating and enforcing decisions throughout (or in certain parts of) the TSFD process.

CHAPTER 4

Challenges and Recommendations Pertaining to the Roles, Responsibilities, and Authorities of Service Implementing Agencies

In coordination with OSD and DSCA, each military department serves as an IA tasked with conducting security cooperation programs and activities, but also establishing policy and guidance and maintaining oversight of service-wide security assistance and security cooperation requirements and activities.[1] Within the context of FMS, this means that the services are responsible both for helping to develop and execute FMS cases and for contributing to the formulation of the rules and procedures for case development and execution. They achieve this through issuing instructions and manuals detailing the roles and responsibilities of service organizations involved in the FMS process and system-specific checklists designed to help ensure that requirements are fully defined and a complete and sustainable capability is delivered to the FMS purchaser. At the apex of the services' loosely bound security assistance structures are SAF/IA, DASA (DE&C), and NIPO. Each of these organizations is configured differently; has different command and reporting relationships with superiors, peers, and subordinates; and possesses somewhat different roles and responsibilities.[2] However, as

---

[1] DSCA, 2012, Chapters 1 and 5; Department of the Army Regulation (AR) 12-1, *Security Assistance, Training and Export Policy*, Headquarters, Department of the Army, 2021, Sections 1 and 2.

[2] SAF/IA has a Deputy Under Secretary of the Air Force for international affairs at its helm, who reports directly to the Under Secretary of the Air Force, whereas the heads of DASA (DE&C) and NIPO are both deputy assistant secretaries who report to the Assistant Secretary of the Army for Acquisition, Logistics and Technology (ASA (ALT)) and the Assistant Secretary of the Navy for Research, Development and Acquisition, respectively. Consequently, SAF/IA has a broader mission set than the other two organizations, encompassing the professional development of U.S. Air Force international airmen, space security cooperation, and security cooperation strategy and enterprise integration, as well as security assistance, armaments cooperation, and technology transfer. For its part, NIPO is a more highly integrated security assistance organization than SAF/IA and DASA (DE&C). NIPO incorporates FMS policy development and case management within the same Navy organization, albeit in different divisions, whereas the Army and Air Force have separate organizations responsible for FMS case management—that is, the U.S. Army Security

principally policy and oversight organizations, they all more or less face the same authorities challenges as DSCA and OSD with respect to FMS implementation, often resorting to establishing "a coalition of the willing" to meet FMS requirements.[3] Furthermore, as noted earlier, the absence of a clear mission for services to support allies and partners means that U.S. acquisition needs will generally be accorded priority over security assistance cases when requirements conflict.[4]

Service-Level Foreign Military Sales Roles, Responsibilities, and Authorities on Paper

According to Department of the Air Force Policy Directive (DAFPD) 16-1, *Operations Support: Security Cooperation*, SAF/IA serves as the Air Force's "focal point" for matters related to the security cooperation enterprise and its activities.[5] This mission includes the following FMS-related responsibilities:

- taking the lead in the Air Force with respect to security cooperation guidance, export policy development, and the development of security cooperation objectives
- synchronizing the execution of security cooperation activities with Air Force activity managers
- serving as the Air Force activity manager for FMS policy and technology transfer and disclosure.

According to AR 12-1, *Security Assistance, Training, and Export Policy*, DASA (DE&C) provides leadership, strategic planning, resource management, and policy for the Army's security assistance enterprise.[6] This role includes

- leading, managing, resourcing, and directing policy and strategy for the conduct of FMS
- engaging and liaising with USD(P), USD(A&S), DSCA, and DTSA regarding areas of responsibility related to FMS
- analyzing, in coordination with all applicable Army offices and agencies, specific requests from foreign countries for defense articles and services

---

Assistance Command (USASAC) and the Army Security Assistance Training Field Activity (SATFA), and the Air Force Security Assistance and Cooperation Directorate (AFSAC) and Air Force Security Assistance Training Squadron (AFSAT). See Secretary of the Air Force International Affairs, homepage, undated; Office of the Deputy Assistant Secretary of the Army for Defense Exports and Cooperation, homepage, undated; and NIPO Portal, homepage, undated.

[3] Navy policy-level official, interview with the authors, July 17, 2023.

[4] DoDD 5100.01, 2020.

[5] DAFPD 16-1, *Operations Support: Security Cooperation*, February 5, 2021.

[6] AR 12-1, 2021.

- supervising the Army's designated lead commands for the execution of their delegated security cooperation responsibilities
- tasking program executive offices (PEOs) and program managers with providing supporting information on weapon systems.

According to its charter, NIPO serves as the principal office for implementing all Department of the Navy international programs concerning security assistance.[7] With respect to FMS, this mission entails

- ensuring all Navy and Coast Guard FMS cases are developed in compliance with DSCA and Navy policy guidance[8]
- in coordination with the Navy Comptroller, developing and allocating the Navy's FMS administrative budget among various Department of the Navy offices with security assistance responsibilities and monitoring budget execution[9]
- serving as executive director of the Technology Transfer and Security Assistance Review Board
- managing participation in international efforts by all Department of the Navy organizational entities with security cooperation program responsibilities.

Service-Level Foreign Military Sales Roles, Responsibilities, and Authorities in Practice

While authorities exist on paper, a common theme that emerged from both policy- and operational-level stakeholders is that these authorities sometimes fall short of what IA leadership need to sufficiently oversee their FMS responsibilities. For example, an Air Force IA official noted there is no ability to "put downward pressure" on the acquisition personnel in organizations outside their chain of command to compel them to speed their involvement in the process.[10]

Some of the most notable examples emanate from Army FMS cases. In particular, DASA (DE&C) has struggled to exert its leadership role, despite Army regulations that mandate the organization's role pertains to guiding, overseeing, allocating resources to, and shaping policy and strategy. The common concern we heard was that subordinate organizations seem to circumvent this authority. One interviewee noted that the organization lacks visibility into the pre-LOR process: "We don't even see the LORs. . . . They go directly from the country to

---

[7] Department of the Navy, *Charter for the Deputy Assistant Secretary of the Navy (International Programs) and Director (Navy International Programs Office)*, December 13, 2007.

[8] NIPOI 4920.3, *Implementation of Foreign Military Sales Case Standard Level of Service Policy Guidance*, Department of the Navy, December 12, 2014.

[9] Department of the Navy, 2007.

[10] Air Force IA official, interview with the authors, February 22, 2023.

USASAC, and if no one tells us about it, we may never see" the case until after the contract is finalized.[11] In one example, DASA (DE&C) requested pre-LOR-related information about a partner from a subordinate organization in preparation for a bilateral defense planning conference only to be told by a subordinate organization, "We do our job and you do yours."[12] In yet another a case, a country desk officer who lacked the "bigger picture" denied the request by a critical strategic partner for an accelerated delivery timeline:

> [A critical partner] asked for accelerated delivery, and a [IA desk officer] said no. We didn't even have insight into that until much later, so we had to figure out how to retract that memo. . . . What was the problem there? [The IA] doesn't have that authority, but [DASA (DE&C)] does not have visibility into LORs on a daily basis. I don't have access to the data portal, and we get them anecdotally from desk officers. For [this] case, [an industry partner] made me aware of it. Where it broke down was that the . . . desk officer felt that they had the authority to say yes and no, but the [regulation] says that that resides at HQ. But it's degraded in recent years.[13]

The action described above was in complete disregard of "denial of request" policy outlined in AR 12-1, which states, "Any proposal to deny a potential FMS customer request must be sent to DASA (DE&C) for review."[14]

DASA (DE&C) is not the only Army organization that expressed concerns regarding insufficient authorities. A stakeholder from a subordinate organization shared that insufficient training within another subordinate entity resulted in employees misinterpreting their roles. Consequently, they turned down tasks that fell within their designated areas of responsibility and created delays in the case as a result.[15] Another IA stakeholder described how an organizational realignment aimed at systems of systems integration requirements has disaggregated roles and responsibilities of the contracting office to an extent that employees are unclear who is responsible for facilitating the overarching FMS case:

> Since we realigned, we divided each piece of the system in different PMs [program managers]. Now we have 6 PMs. The contract piece now has the problem of who's going to handle the contract? Even though you said OK, but you can separate it and you get your piece but at the end, as far as contracts, you're going to have like how many contracts? 4 instead of 1. We are at the challenge right now trying to decide from a higher level who's going to have what contract.[16]

---

[11] Army IA official, interview with the authors, June 2, 2023.

[12] Army IA official, interview with the authors, June 2, 2023.

[13] Army IA official, interview with the authors, June 2, 2023.

[14] According to AR 12-1, 3-6, DASA (DE&C) does not have the final word on FMS proposals. That decision lies with DSCA.

[15] Army IA stakeholder, interview with the authors, April 21, 2023.

[16] Army IA stakeholder, interview with the authors, April 24, 2023.

Yet another stakeholder highlighted that there is no single entity or person responsible for overseeing all the different Army organizations that need to work together, making it challenging to establish clear lines of authority and accountability within the service.

> Everyone is working in a vacuum and doing their own thing. It's like wrangling cats. . . . There is no one entity that owns all the agencies that are required to respond. There are so many agencies in the Army's SA [security assistance] enterprise. I have no authority or mechanism to hold someone accountable for being unresponsive or for failing. . . . It makes it very tough and requires really strong relationships.[17]

The cumulative effect of these issues across various echelons is that the Army enterprise has developed a reputation for insufficient authorities and a general sense of a lack of accountability. As one Army IA official noted,

> The Army is perceived as slow and lethargic in responding to international demands and meeting the needs of partners. We are failing on integrated defense because we take too long to build cases and execute with the right quality. It's only 10–15% cases that fall into that issue, but those are the high-profile ones. The higher ups don't feel like they have any insight or control into SC execution.[18]

When it comes to FMS case execution, SAF/IA and NIPO face a similar challenge (though the examples we heard were far less egregious than those coming from the Army). According to one OSD interviewee, these organizations "don't actually have real authority over the [acquisition] program offices" in the services' systems commands.[19] In SAF/IA's case, they lack tasking authority over PEOs and Life Cycle System Commands that manage acquisition projects for the Air Force. "If SAF/IA wants something done" with respect to the execution of an FMS case, "it has to go all the way up to the Chief of Staff of the Air Force and then all the way back down to the PEO."[20]

It is important to note that not all service security assistance commands and program offices we spoke with shared the perspective that insufficient authorities were at the root of issues negatively affecting FMS deliveries. According to one interviewee, the primary challenge to delivering material solutions to partner nations in support of the CCMDs is not a lack of authority on the part of IAs; rather, it is lack of resources on the part of case and program managers to do what they have been asked to do by various FMS stakeholders. The problems faced by this stakeholder's organization are a numbers game:

> We're resource constrained like everyone else. Looking back 5–6 years, case numbers keep going up. We've already exceeded last year's total and this year new business is $22.5 billion and we're projecting $30 billion by the end of the year. . . . This is all to illustrate that

[17] Army IA stakeholder, interview with the authors, March 17, 2023.

[18] Army IA official, interview with the authors, June 2, 2023.

[19] OSD official, interview with the authors, May 18, 2023.

[20] DSCA official, interview with the authors, February 9, 2023.

> workload and money is going up, but my budget is stagnant, which limits my abilities to bring on more workforce and contractors.[21]

As a result of being understaffed and overworked, offices tasked to accelerate the process make mistakes that lead to the opposite effect, as one Army IA stakeholder recounted:

> Sometimes these situations are high speed. You get that pressure from above to get stuff done quickly. When you get things done quickly, you miss things. So, it'll get up to CWD [Case Writing Division] and they say you forgot to do this waiver, or you forgot to put this note in there. It's not necessarily major things that we've missed, it's just working too fast. . . . We're trying to develop things along the way. If CWD had something they could share that would be amazing.[22]

A Navy IA official expressed similar concerns, describing challenges personnel experience when accessing contracting information due to the lack of technical capacity to meet the multitude of emergent and urgent requests for information:

> A lot of the things are data calls and what's in the art of the possible and given everything that's happening globally that could be any number of things. One of the recent examples is having someone from [ ] contact us and say there's this meeting in a couple of days the Admiral needs this information and can we get it by tomorrow. What you're asking for is information that would come from probably 10 or 12 different program management offices; this isn't something that they have readily off the shelf. You're asking them to create new content and you're asking them to stop and take time to report specific set of data in a specific format and you need it by tomorrow. I understand it's for the Admiral, but you could have asked for this information probably two weeks ago. It's waiting to ask us and then us pushing back saying we can't do this in 24 hours. We need about a week.[23]

Whether a lack of adequate resources is the issue or not, mistakes can have deleterious effects. One DSCA stakeholder described a situation where a mistake by a Navy implementer ultimately led to cost increases for the partner:

> There could be a budgeting problem. Or something will get approved that probably shouldn't get approved. Then, it takes them forever to address it and now the customers have to pay more for something that the customer never expected that they'd have to pay for. That's one of the challenges with FMS is that we can't lose money. If there's an error on the case and something comes back more expensive, 9 times out of 10 the customer is going to have to pay for that. That's just how FMS works. But you can't delay news. You have to give that news in a timely manner and delaying it just makes it worse.[24]

---

[21] Army IA official, interview with the authors, May 30, 2023.

[22] Army IA official, interview with the authors, April 21, 2023.

[23] Navy IA official, interview with the authors, April 4, 2023.

[24] DSCA official, interview with the authors, May 2, 2023.

We were not able to gain insights into whether disconnects in authorities, manpower constraints, or mistakes that result in confusion or delays were a systematic issue, nor whether they had a lasting impact on partners' experiences with the FMS process. However, it is not unreasonable to assume that such issues, if not remedied, could negatively affect a partner's future purchasing decisions.

Service Implementing Agency Recommendations

Much like DSCA, SAF/IA, DASA (DE&C), and NIPO lack authority to compel other organizations within their MILDEPs to follow their case development policies and provide status information on FMS proposals and cases. For SAF/IA and DASA (DE&C), these other organizations include security assistance commands responsible for case management, like AFSAC/AFSAT and USASAC/SATFA,[25] as well as systems and life-cycle commands and program offices responsible for acquiring the defense articles for DoD and foreign customers. Because NIPO is responsible for both FMS policy development and case management, its authority is restricted primarily to the realm of acquisition. To increase the authority of top-level IA organizations over other MILDEP organizations involved in FMS implementation, we recommend adjustments to service-specific military regulations.

Service regulations give leading DoD security assistance organizations enforcement authority in areas they are responsible for overseeing and managing. Each service headquarters and some subordinate commands issue these regulations to govern the conduct, duties, responsibilities, and operations of military personnel within that branch. This guidance is an essential component of military discipline and ensures that service members adhere to the standards and expectations of their respective services. Military personnel are required to comply with service regulations, and failure to do so can result in disciplinary actions, including reprimands, administrative actions, and, in more severe cases, court-martial proceedings. Assuming senior leaders are committed to holding personnel accountable to adhering to its policies, our research suggests amendments to several of these documents could enhance service-specific FMS case roles and responsibilities to include the following:

- The Air Force and Army modify DAFPD 16-1 and AR 12-1, respectively, to permit SAF/IA and DASA (DE&C) to participate in the process of selecting top leaders at AFSAC/AFSAT and USASAC/SATFA.
- The Air Force, Army, and Navy modify DAFPD 16-1, AR 12-1, and the NIPO charter, respectively, to enable SAF/IA, DASA (DE&C), and NIPO to provide periodic evaluations of FMS case development and execution performance within their domains to MILDEP leaders, as well as DSCA, USD(P), and USD(A&S).

[25] AFSAC falls under the Air Force Life Cycle Management Command, which falls under Air Force Materiel Command (a U.S. Air Force Major Command [MAJCOM]), a principal case-writing IA organization; AFSAT falls under the Air Education & Training Command (MAJCOM) and is also a principal case-writing IA organization.

TABLE 4.1

Recommended Changes to Guidance to Increase the Authority of Leading Department of Defense Foreign Military Sales Implementation Organizations

Authorities Challenge	Recommended Change in Authority
Air Force and Army FMS case management organizations fall outside the "line authority" of SAF/IA and DASA (DE&C).	• Amend DAFPD 16-1 and AR 12-1 to state that SAF/IA and DASA (DE&C) will participate in the process of selecting top leaders at AFSAC/AFSAT and USASAC/SATFA, respectively.
SAF/IA, DASA (DE&C), and NIPO lack administrative control over the security assistance activities of MILDEP acquisition organizations.	• Amend DAFPD 16-1, AR 12-1, and the NIPO charter to state that SAF/IA, DASA (DE&C), and NIPO will provide periodic evaluations of MILDEP security assistance and systems command FMS case development and execution performance to their MILDEP leadership, as well as DSCA, USD(P), and USD(A&S).

Table 4.1 summarizes the authorities challenges and recommendations for addressing them.

As this chapter has described, many of the challenges the IAs experience are outside the span of control of IA leadership (i.e., obsolete systems, involvement of other government organizations). And similar to the enhanced authorities we have recommended for DSCA, granting SAF/IA, DASA (DE&C), and NIPO the authority to help select the leaders of security assistance organizations and evaluate the performance of security assistance and acquisition organizations will likely not be a silver-bullet solution for increasing the efficiency and effectiveness of service case development processes. Nevertheless, fostering a security assistance–minded culture starts at the top (or at least across the dotted-line hierarchy),[26] and providing the IA leadership a say in that process may influence the services regarding decisions on personnel recruitment, professional development, and training in their security assistance organizations, as well as improvements to their data and reporting systems that allow for proposal and case tracking across different phases of the FMS process and for sharing inside and outside their MILDEPs.

---

[26] A SAF/IA stakeholder described the organizational and largely collaborative relationship between SAF/IA and relevant security assistance organizations and somewhat pushed back on our recommendation regarding the benefits of increasing SAF/IA's influence over these organizations, noting that "SAF/IA has dotted-line policy and program management authority over and shared between AFSAC, AFSAT, and Program Offices executing FMS cases, governs and enables SAF/IA to work through case execution and acquisitions issues. SAF/IA is also a Headquarters Air Force Staff Secretariat [that] works alongside SAF/AQ Air Force Acquisitions and regularly liaises with Staff level acquisition counterparts to address issues that rise to the Staff level. Additionally, SAF/IA's role and position with the HAF [Headquarters Air Force] allows SAF/IA to directly address SA/SC issues with the Chief Staff and is a considered added benefit."

CHAPTER 5

Complex, Duplicative Roles and Responsibilities in the Army Security Assistance Enterprise

In Chapters 2–4 we discussed ways in which insufficient authorities or failure to exert existing authorities were major sources of concern across strategic, operational, and tactical levels of the FMS enterprise. In this chapter we highlight another issue of concern raised in the exploratory phase of our research: the risk of duplication or redundant roles that can slow the FMS process. The study team conducted a rigorous RRA analysis outlined in FMS guidance with an aim to reconcile stakeholder perceptions with the actual policies themselves. The team found only a few roles with any overlap, with only one having a significant impact on the FMS process: the different case management entities in the MILDEPs. And nowhere was this more pronounced than in the Army FMS enterprise, which stakeholders described as being plagued by redundancy and sluggishness and lacking due course for accountability for delays in case processing.

This chapter will provide a case study of this role duplication across the case management entities in the IAs focused specifically on the Army, as well as provide several recommendations the Army can consider as it looks to ameliorate these issues.

Service Case Manager Roles

To better understand the root causes of these issues, the team examined the case management roles and responsibilities across the MILDEPs to look for any commonality or differences that may explain these results. The SAMM clearly lays out the roles and responsibilities of the IA case managers (CMs) throughout the FMS process as the IA entity "to assist with case development, and to guide execution of the case after implementation."[1] The SAMM includes a full list of the responsibilities of the IA CM:

1. Serve as the central point of contact for matters related to the case. Establish and publish initial and long-range goals, objectives, and plans for case management and

[1] DSCA, 2012, C2.2.1.

execution. Issue and maintain a program master plan with key program milestones as the case is implemented.

2. Ensure program goals and objectives are in accordance with approved foreign disclosure and technology transfer requirements.
3. Consider customer transportation preferences during LOA development. Ensure transportation documents are in place (transportation plan, Communications Interoperability and Security Memorandum of Agreement, etc.).
4. Ensure contracting milestones are met.
5. Ensure appropriate integration of requirements such as supply requisitions, contracts, and training are accomplished with internal and external organizations.
6. Ensure funding is in place and financial requirements are met.
7. Ensure material and services performance is met in relation to required performance specifications. Ensure that appropriate actions are taken to maintain accountability of training events, to include Defense Security Assistance Management System—Training Module entry.
8. Ensure that delivery and performance reports are timely and accurate. Check that automated records and data sources, such as Security Cooperation Information Portal, reflect accurate information.
9. Maintain a case file of significant events, documents, and decisions. Ensure that case records are retained for a period of 10 years after final closure in accordance with DoD 7000.14-R, *Department of Defense Financial Management Regulation (DoD FMR)*, Volume 15, Chapter 6.
10. Reconcile the case throughout its life cycle starting with implementation and prepare the case for closure.
11. Become familiar with policies, management information systems, internal and external organizational elements, and the stages of the FMS process.[2]

Although the SAMM specifies the tasks that an IA CM must fulfill, it leaves room for interpretation regarding how an IA will carry out these functions.[3] There is wide variation between the IAs, especially the MILDEPs, in how case management is organized and what responsibilities specific case management entities have. Table 5.1 summarizes the most relevant organizations and their associated roles.

The team compared the CM roles outlined in the SAMM with the roles of various security assistance managers across the services to determine if role duplication exists among these positions. The results are shown in Table 5.2, which indicates in bold text where there is extensive overlap between case management responsibilities for several entities in each of the three MILDEPs.

---

[2] DSCA, 2012, Table C2.T1.

[3] DSCA, 2012, C2.2.1.

TABLE 5.1
Mapping Military Department Case Management Entities

Management Level	Air Force	Navy	Army
Policy Management	SAF/IA	NIPO	DASA (DE&C)
Country Portfolio Management	SAF/IA country director (CD)	NIPO country program director (CPD)	USASAC/SATFA country portfolio manager
Case Management	AFSAC/AFSAT command country manager (CCM)[a]	U.S. Navy Systems Command (SYSCOM) CM	USASAC/SATFA central case manager
Case Development	AFSAC/AFSAT CM	SYSCOM CM	Life Cycle Management Command (LCMC) Security Assistance Management Directorate (SAMD)
Line Management	MAJCOM or PEO line manager (LM)	SYSCOM CM	PEO

SOURCES: RAND analysis of Defense Security Cooperation Agency, 2012, Table C2.T1; DA PAM 12-1, *Security Assistance Procedures and Operations*, Headquarters, Department of the Army, 2016; Air Force Manual 16-101, *Security Cooperation (SC) and Security Assistance (SA) Management*, Department of the Air Force, 2018; Department of the Navy, *NAVYIPOINST 4920.1D: Foreign Military Sales Case Development Manual*, Department of the Navy, 2021.

[a] To reduce complexity, we have left the Air Force security assistance program manager (SAPM) out of this table. The SAPM fulfills a similar role to the AFSAC/AFSAT CCM, but for major or complex system sales crossing one or more program offices. SAPMs are government acquisition personnel and are assigned to divisions within a program office, headed by a senior material lead, and under a directorate led by a program executive officer.

TABLE 5.2
Case Manager Responsibilities by Military Department

SAMM Case Manager Responsibilities	Army	Air Force	Navy
Serves as central point of contact for case-related matters	CPM[a]	**CD CM CCM**	**CM CPD**
Establishes and publishes initial and long-range goals, objectives, and plans for case management and execution	CPM	**CD CM**	**CM CPD**
Issues and maintains a program master plan with key program milestones as the case is implemented	CCM	**CM CCM**	CM
Ensures program goals and objectives are in accordance with approved foreign disclosure and technology transfer requirements	CPM	CCM	CM
Considers customer transportation preferences during LOA development and ensures that transportation documents are in place	**CPM SAMD**	CCM	CM
Ensures contracting milestones	**CPM CCM SAMD**	**CD CM CCM**	CM
Ensures appropriate integration of requirements	CPM	CM	CM
Ensures funding is in place and financial requirements are met	**CPM SAMD**	CM	CM

Table 5.2—Continued

SAMM Case Manager Responsibilities	Army	Air Force	Navy
Ensures material and services performance is met in relation to required performance specifications and ensures that appropriate actions are taken to maintain accountability of training events	**CCM** **SAMD**	CD	CM
Ensures that delivery and performance reports are timely and accurate, and checks that automated records and data sources, such as Security Cooperation Information Portal, reflect accurate information	CPM	CM	CM
Maintains a case file of significant events, documents, and decisions, and retains records for ten years	**CPM** **CCM**	CM	**CM** **CPD**
Reconciles the case throughout its lifecycle starting with implementation and prepares the case for closure	SAMD	CM	CM

SOURCE: RAND analysis of DSCA, 2012, Table C2.T1; DA PAM 12-1, 2016; Air Force Manual 16-101, 2018; Department of the Navy, 2021.

[a] CPM = country program manager

Although all the services have multiple entities fulfilling the roles and responsibilities of the CM as defined in the SAMM, the team rarely heard interviewees mention duplication causing issues for the Air Force and Navy FMS enterprises.[4] The same cannot be said for the Army, and both Army and other interviewees have described the issues caused by lack of a centralized case authority and several overlapping entities viewing themselves as responsible for the various CM tasks outlined in the SAMM.

Army Foreign Military Sales Enterprise on Paper

Army FMS case management responsibilities are spread out between a variety of organizational levels and commands. The first level of Army FMS case management includes USASAC, SATFA, and the U.S. Army Corps of Engineers (USACE). USASAC falls under Army Materiel Command (AMC) and oversees defense articles, as well as training and technical support outside the continental United States. SATFA falls under United States Army Training and Doctrine Command and oversees continental U.S.–based training and technical assistance

[4] Air Force IA stakeholder, interview with the authors, February 14, 2023; Air Force IA stakeholder, interview with the authors, February 22, 2023; Air Force IA stakeholder, interview with the authors, April 4, 2023; Air Force IA stakeholder, interview with the authors, April 6, 2023; Air Force IA stakeholder, interview with the authors, June 13, 2023; Navy IA stakeholder, interview with the authors, June 8, 2023; Navy IA stakeholder, interview with the authors, July 17, 2023; Navy IA stakeholder, interview with the authors, March 3, 2023; Navy IA stakeholder, interview with the authors, February 15, 2023; Navy IA stakeholder, interview with the authors, March 26, 2023; Navy IA stakeholder, interview with the authors, May 26, 2023.

programs. USACE oversees construction cases. All three agencies, according to AR 12-1, are responsible for the following tasks, among many others:

- receiving, processing, and executing FMS requests
- providing centralized financial management for those programs under their purview.[5]

USASAC is also specifically responsible for

- providing financial management and distribution of FMS administrative funds to the LCMCs
- managing FMS case funds
- establishing and maintaining case and program management systems
- conducting periodic reviews
- reporting on the state of materiel and training activities.[6]

As stated in the previous section, USASAC and SATFA provide the CPMs for the Army's FMS enterprise. USASAC/SATFA CPMs have overall managerial responsibility for security cooperation programs in their designated countries and their designated programs during the pre-LOR and case development phases and fulfill the following roles:

- acting as a point of contact to partners and the interagency
- tasking the appropriate entities to write the LOA or price and availability
- overseeing program execution
- conducting quality control for case documents
- coordinating between the various FMS entities in the Army
- serving as the customer advocate for the Army.[7]

USASAC also provides CCMs to the Army FMS process. CCMs are tasked with overall responsibility for case execution from implementation to closure and fulfill the following roles:

- ensuring the LOA is executed on schedule and within the budget
- developing the case master plan
- providing financial analysis and LOA status reports
- scheduling periodic LOA reviews
- integrating actions assigned to other FMS entities
- tracking and documenting all significant activities encountered during execution and closure.[8]

[5] AR 12-1, 2021, pp. 10–11.

[6] AR 12-1, 2021, p. 10.

[7] DA PAM 12-1, 2016, p. 122.

[8] DA PAM 12-1, 2016, p. 123.

The next layer of case management for Army FMS enterprise is the SAMD, which belong to the various LCMCs under AMC. The SAMD, designated by the Army as the case-preparing activity, assigns an international program manager (IPM) who is responsible for writing the case itself,[9] as well as

- working in coordination with the USASAC CCM to ensure overall case execution tasks are met
- providing technical advice to the partner and the interagency
- ensuring that case data are tracked and logged
- ensuring that material is acquired and released on schedule and within program parameters.[10]

The SAMD IPM works closely on case writing with the PEOs, who report directly to Assistant Secretary of the Army (Acquisition, Logistics, and Technology) (ASA (ALT)) through the U.S. Army Acquisition Support Center. The PEO program manager is the technical expert on the equipment itself. Program managers assist the IPMs in developing requirements and taking necessary actions to ensure cases are meeting their timelines and budgets. Unlike the other case management entities described above, who are only responsible for security assistance cases, PEOs are also responsible for U.S. Army equipping as well.

DASA (DE&C), under ASA (ALT), is also an integral part of the Army FMS enterprise. Its roles and responsibilities, as the Department of the Army's representation, are leading, managing, resourcing, and directing Army security cooperation strategy and policy, as well as ensuring that "security cooperation programs are conducted according to law and policy" and providing support and enable inter- and intra-agency coordination.[11] DASA (DE&C) also assists USASAC with waivers, TSFD, and disclosures before they are passed to DSCA.[12] Although DASA (DE&C) does not have a case management role, it is responsible for the execution of country plans and strategies that often include FMS.

Army Roles, Responsibilities, and Authorities in Practice

The ways in which Army guidance structures and guides Army FMS can cloud and stymie the process in myriad ways. Interviewees reported that getting responses to inquiries from the various levels of the Army FMS enterprise is a frustrating and time-consuming experience. One Army stakeholder told the study team that "the Army is perceived as slow and lethargic in responding to international demands and meeting the needs of partners,"[13] and

---

9 Army IA stakeholder, interview with the authors, March 17, 2023.

10 DA PAM 12-1, 2016, p. 123.

11 AR 12-1, 2021, pp. 5–8.

12 Army IA stakeholder, interview with the authors, February 28, 2023.

13 Army IA stakeholder, interview with the authors, June 2, 2023.

another described the process of responding to partner inquiries as "a game of telephone."[14] Based on interviews and the mapping exercise, this slowness is due to an overly complex case management structure, multiple chains of command creating complex communication channels, and a lack of central authority.

DA PAM 12-1 provides an extensive overview of the roles and responsibilities of each of the case management entities listed in the previous section, but as Figure 5.1 illustrates, it creates a complex, multilayered structure with two central players, the USASAC CPM and the SAMD IPM.[15] The document gives the CPM "oversight responsibility for total SA program management and all associated actions through case closure,"[16] while also stating that "the SAMDs manage FMS program milestones and scheduling dates pertaining to their support products and services."[17] According to our research and analysis, this creates a situation where both consider themselves the central coordinator for cases and the other to

FIGURE 5.1
Army Foreign Military Sales Case Development Process per Department of the Army Pamphlet 12-1

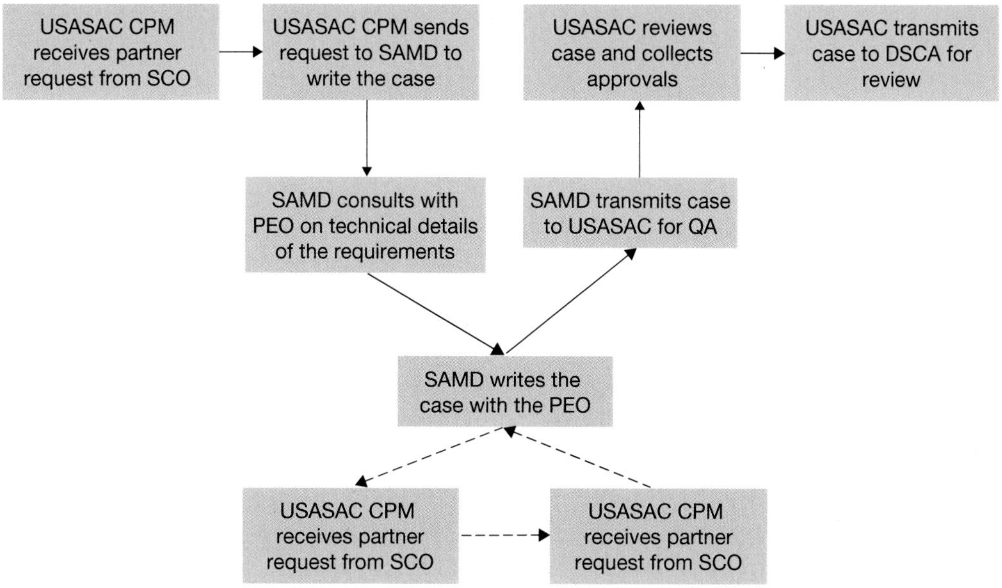

SOURCE: RAND analysis of process described in DA PAM 12-1, 2016.
NOTE: QA = quality assurance.

[14] Army IA stakeholder, interview with the authors, April 3, 2023.

[15] Although SATFA and USACE are also central players in case development, specifically for continental U.S.–based training/technical assistance and construction, respectively, the team did not receive reports of overlapping responsibility issues regarding SATFA or USACE during interviews or document reviews.

[16] DA PAM 12-1, 2016, p. 17.

[17] DA PAM 12-1, 2016, p. 19.

be the middleman who just passes information along from the partner to the PEO.[18] Conversely, as described in some interviews, with these duplicative roles, it may be difficult for complex cases to get one to commit to taking on the lead role as the CM.[19]

Additionally, the FMS case management structure itself creates complex lines of communication that can slow down the process. In an ideal case, as shown above, the USASAC CPM should receive a partner request from the SCOs, which is then passed down to the SAMD to write the case. The SAMD would then coordinate with the PEO or project manager to write the case, as the program subject-matter experts are located in the PEO. Any questions for the partner or interagency would be routed up through the SAMD to USASAC, before heading back down the same chain with the answer. Even this ideal system creates a point of failure in facilitating efficient communications with the partner, and in many cases the efficient passing of information is reliant on the specific individuals involved.[20]

At the same time, based on our interviews, this ideal process is rarely the reality. In actuality, the partner request can enter the Army FMS system through any point in the enterprise: directly to the CPM, the SAMD, the PEO, DASA (DE&C), and so on. The point of entry depends heavily on the partner's past relationships with the Army and how well the partner knows how to play the system.[21] This too can create confusion, as not all the information will make its way to those who need to be in the know.

Furthermore, as shown in Figure 5.1, DASA (DE&C) is not included in many of these communication loops. As discussed in Chapter 2 of AR 12-1, DASA (DE&C) is responsible for leading, managing, resourcing, and directing Army security cooperation strategy and policy, as well as ensuring that "security cooperation programs are conducted according to law and policy."[22] The policy-level organization has a difficult time getting case status updates from both the SAMD and USASAC, who fall under AMC. Instead, DASA (DE&C) will often go directly to the PEO because both report to ASA (ALT). Although it may be faster to get the answer in this manner, it can cut other entities out of the communication loop entirely. This can result in the Army not speaking with the partner in a unified voice,[23] and in some cases, could lead to other Army FMS entities making unilateral strategic policy decisions regarding what equipment a country can get without DASA (DE&C)'s involvement or even visibility into the decision being made.[24]

---

[18] Army IA stakeholder, interview with the authors, April 21, 2023; Army IA stakeholder, interview with the authors, February 28, 2023.

[19] SCO member, interview with the authors, March 14, 2023.

[20] DSCA stakeholder, interview with the authors, March 13, 2023.

[21] DSCA stakeholder, interview with the authors, March 13, 2023.

[22] AR 12-1, 2021, p. 5.

[23] Army IA stakeholder, interview with the authors, June 2, 2023.

[24] Army IA stakeholder, interview with the authors, June 2, 2023.

As alluded to above, this is further exacerbated by the fact that the different case management entities fall under different chains of command, and each lacks the authority to hold other entities accountable in responding and reporting in a timely manner.

Army Security Assistance Enterprise Reform Effort

The Army is currently undertaking an effort to reform its security assistance enterprise using the FMS Tiger Team's analysis, internal Army analysis, and DoS's 10-point action plan.[25] The Army Security Assistance Enterprise (ASAE) developed six lines of effort (LOEs); two of these LOEs, LOE 2 and LOE 3, are intended to address the issues outlined in the analysis above.[26] Below is a further description of these LOEs.

- LOE 2—Roles and Responsibilities: Roles and responsibilities not clearly defined between ASAE elements, creating duplication of activities. Confusion exists among external stakeholders on decision authorities, execution, and coordination.
- LOE 3—Processes and Governance: Unique, local policies and processes exist among each command, resulting in siloed execution; there is no singular forum to align leadership on ASAE performance.

This reform effort is still in its early stages, but objectives and recommended leads have been identified for each LOE. ASA (ALT) and G-3/5/7 have been recommended to lead LOE 2, and its objectives are to

- codify roles and responsibilities across ASAE elements and identify duplicative efforts across enterprises
- issue policies and regulations, revisiting roles and responsibilities as required to support execution.

USASAC has been recommended to lead LOE 3, and its objectives are to

- analyze the LOR-to-LOA process and provide recommendations for immediate process improvement
- overhaul end-to-end LOR-to-LOA process.

According to planning documents, at the time of this report writing in the summer of 2023, the Army was in the process of finalizing Phase 1, which was focused on short-term outcomes, and had plans to start Phase 2 in October 2023, which was expected to focus "on broader structural, policy and process adjustments."[27]

---

[25] See U.S. Army, *Army Security Assistance Enterprise (ASAE) Reform*, 2023.

[26] Other LOEs include LOE 1, Strategy, Statute, Regulations, and Policy; LOE 4, Data and Analytics; LOE 5, Technology Security and Foreign Disclosure; and LOE 6, Workforce Development.

[27] U.S. Army, 2023, slide 7.

Army Suggestions

As the ASAE continues with its reform efforts, it will need to find ways to simplify its FMS processes, eliminate overly complex communication channels, and reconnect incongruent chains of command to address the issues explored above. Based on the findings of this report, we can provide the Army with several suggestions to consider as it proceeds, including clarifying the separation between case management roles and condensing or realigning CM responsibilities and authority within the ASAE.

Clarify Roles and Responsibilities

The Army should clarify the language it uses to describe the roles and responsibilities of the USASAC CPM, and the SAMD in DA PAM 12-1, specifically regarding case development in Chapter 4. The document grants duplicative management oversight of case execution to the CPM, the SAMD, and the CCM.[28] Additionally, toward the end of the document—Chapter 18—DA PAM includes general roles and responsibilities for many of the case management roles, including the CPM, CCM, and SAMD. This chapter should be moved to the front of the document to provide readers clear definitions of each case management entity's overall role in FMS before providing additional detail about roles in individual processes. The document could also benefit from clearer differentiation of the hierarchical levels of oversight and coordination authorities between the three entities by describing who has the central authority for holding others accountable.

Condense Army Foreign Military Sales Enterprise

In addition to clarifying language, the Army might consider making structural changes and reallocating some roles and responsibilities to reduce complexity in the Army FMS enterprise. The team has developed several options for the Army to consider while it proceeds with its reforms.

Approach 1

One approach would be to absorb the USASAC CPM's portfolio management responsibilities into DASA (DE&C). These would specifically include the CPM's role as "the principal manager for all SA programs related to the assigned country," as well as the role as the overall country point of contact and customer advocate. This would enable DASA (DE&C) to maintain international policy control and fulfill its responsibilities for leading and managing FMS

[28] DA PAM 12-1, p. 17, states, "The CPM has oversight responsibility for total SA program management and all associated actions through case closure. This includes ensuring that all case milestones are managed during case development and execution." Page 19 states that "the SAMDs manage FMS program milestones and scheduling dates pertaining to their supported products and services." Page 123 states, "The CCM, in coordination with the SAMD IPM, is responsible for overall case execution from date of implementation through closure while the PM is responsible for program execution."

policy and strategy, ensuring that programs are conducted according to the law and policy, and resolving security assistance policy issues for specific country programs.[29] This would not only place DASA (DE&C) inside the FMS case development loop and give the policy organization administrative control over the process, in accordance with its mandate in AR 12-1, but would also remove one layer of complexity in the ASAE.

In this approach, the CCM role should remain in USASAC so that it, as the designated AMC representative, can fulfill its responsibility for establishing and maintaining a case and program management system,[30] as well as processing and executing FMS materiel and technical assistance requests. This would leave information management, financial policy, and logistical guidance in USASAC.

Approach 2

Another approach would be to absorb the SAMD's case-writing expertise into the PEO. Multiple interviewees told us that although the SAMD is responsible for writing the FMS case, they must consult with the PEO, as the SAMD does not contain the technical expertise on the individual materiel and systems to write cases on its own. Merging the case-writing responsibilities into the PEO would eliminate a layer of complexity in the case development process. As the PEO is also responsible for acquisition support for U.S. Army systems as well, this recommendation would require international CM personnel in the PEOs to handle specifically the FMS case-writing requests.

Downsides to Approaches 1 and 2

The downside of each of these approaches is that each one eliminates an AMC touchpoint with the FMS process. Both USASAC and the SAMD, through the LCMC, report to AMC, while both DASA (DE&C) and the PEOs report to ASA (ALT). By AR 12-1, AMC is still responsible for receiving, processing, and executing partner requests.[31] Although there is some duplication between the CPM and the SAMD, eliminating both positions would leave AMC without a way to fulfill its responsibilities.

Approach 3

If the Army is examining a radical restructuring of its security assistance enterprise, a third approach would be to combine the roles and responsibilities of the CPM, CCM, and the SAMD into a single entity, residing in either USASAC or the LCMC. This new, unified entity would be responsible for country program management, case preparation, and case management. The position would still require the technical expertise of PEOs to prepare and execute the case, but a combined entity would eliminate several layers of complexity in case management.

---

[29] AR 12-1, 2021, p. 5.

[30] AR 12-1, 2021, p. 10.

[31] AR 12-1, 2021, pp. 10–11.

TABLE 5.3
Army-Specific Challenges and Recommendations Pertaining to Roles, Responsibilities, and Authorities

Challenge	Recommendation
Duplicative or redundant roles can slow the FMS process; this is a particular issue within Army FMS case management.	• The Army should clarify the duplicative language it uses to describe the roles and responsibilities of the USASAC CPM and the SAMD in DA PAM 12-1. • The Army might consider structural changes to better streamline processes.

The Navy's security assistance enterprise could provide a helpful model for its reform efforts. The Navy houses all of its security assistance entities, NIPO (the Navy equivalent of both DASA [DE&C] and USASAC), the SYSCOMs (the Navy equivalent of the LCMCs), and the PEOs, under the same chain of command: the Assistant Secretary of the Navy for Research, Development, and Acquisition.[32] Even though there is overlap in some of the roles and responsibilities between specific case management entities, placing both under the same chain of command ensures that the Navy has a clear line of communication, authority, and accountability in its FMS enterprise. Table 5.3 summarizes our recommendations.

[32] Assistant Secretary of the Navy for RDA, "ASN(RDA) Overall Structure," webpage, undated.

CHAPTER 6

Conclusion

The 2022 National Defense Strategy devotes an entire chapter to underscoring the significance of partners and allies in attaining U.S. national defense goals. The document describes the strategy as "a call to action for the defense enterprise to incorporate allies and partners at every stage of defense planning."[1] FMS plays an integral role in building partner military capabilities that can work toward that call, yet a wide range of factors can sometimes make it challenging for stakeholder organizations to carry out FMS processes and commitments in a timely fashion.

It is important to note that most cases are delivered on time and as expected, and those that experience complications are typically resolved after senior leader intervention. Given the procedural and organizational complexity of FMS, it is perhaps surprising that FMS implementation works as well as it does. These achievements are likely due to a combination of factors, including a dedicated security assistance workforce and leadership, a willingness of many stakeholders to coordinate and collaborate with one another, and an established and interconnected FMS process buttressed by detailed policies and regulations, not to mention the top-quality U.S. defense articles and services that foreign partners can procure via FMS. Still, numerous prior FMS reform efforts attest to a high degree of dissatisfaction on the part of stakeholders with the way FMS are being carried out. And the increased demand for advanced military equipment in recent years has made this situation ever more challenging.

In recognition of the criticality of the FMS implementation problem, the Deputy Secretary of Defense launched a high-level Tiger Team initiative in 2022 to uncover new and lasting ways of improving the efficiency and effectiveness of the FMS process. As we explained in the introduction, RAND's study of FMS RRAs is an adjunct to this larger effort. On the one hand, the Deputy Secretary of Defense's request for an independent, focused examination of RRAs is an acknowledgment of the politically loaded nature of this topic, given the array of organizations involved in security assistance. On the other hand, it also reflects the importance of clear and comprehensive RRAs to reforming the FMS process so that it aligns with a changed international security environment.

---

[1] DoD, 2022, p. 14.

Summary of Challenges and Recommendations Pertaining to Foreign Military Sales, Roles, Responsibilities, and Authorities

One of the points that was made early on in RAND's discussions and interviews with officials at DSCA was the perceived imbalance between DSCA's responsibilities in the area of FMS implementation and the authorities necessary to ensure efficient and effective implementation. Our research found that the problem is not a complete lack of authority: DSCA has policy and resourcing authority over many, though not all, aspects of FMS implementation and associated workforce development. However, it lacks "line" authority to direct FMS case development and, especially, the case execution, as well as to hold service IAs and SCOs accountable for their FMS responsibilities. Furthermore, DSCA's dilemma is shared with other leading security assistance organizations, including DoS, OSD, DTSA, and the service secretariats. Operational-level organizations experience pain points, and personnel with FMS roles and responsibilities contend with diffuse and obscure guidance. The combined impact is an FMS process that is at times suboptimal for meeting its partner purchasing commitments.

The study team investigated ways that the enforcement authority of leading DoD security assistance organizations could be enhanced. We are recommending that this enhancement begin with amending DoDDs and service regulations that prescribe the key RRAs of these organizations. We also provide a couple of suggestions geared toward improvements in the Army's FMS enterprise specifically in recognition that the service is currently undergoing its own review and may benefit from our tangential assessment.

We summarize the key challenges we identified and our recommendations for addressing them in Table 6.1.

TABLE 6.1
Summary of Challenges and Recommendations Pertaining to Foreign Military Sales Roles, Responsibilities, and Authorities

Challenge	Recommendation
Recent recommendations to SECDEF to increase DSCA's administrative control over SCOs' workforce to improve personnel training, qualifications, and performance do not include modifications to DSCA's RRAs in DoDDs.	• Amend DoDD 5132.03 and/or DoDD 5105.65 to state that all personnel selected for SCO assignments shall be transferred to DSCA administrative control for training before taking up their assignments; additionally, DSCA will have approving authority over all SCO billet descriptions and, where appropriate, SCO chief selections. DSCA will also recommend FMS-related criteria that should be addressed in SCO chief evaluations.
DSCA lacks the authority to hold service IA officials accountable for failing to meet case development timelines and standards and to keep it apprised of problems related to major FMS proposals and cases.	• Amend DoDD 5132.03 and/or DoDD 5105.65 to state that the director of DSCA will participate in the process of selecting top leaders at SAF/IA, DASA (DE&C), and NIPO and will provide periodic evaluations of IAs' FMS case development performance to OSD-P and MILDEP leaders.

Table 6.1—Continued

Challenge	Recommendation
DSCA lacks the authority to require MILDEP contracting and acquisition officials to provide periodic updates on the status of security assistance–related cases.	• Amend DoDD 5105.65 to state that the MILDEPs have the responsibility for providing accurate and up-to-date information to DSCA, OUSD(P), and OUSD(A&S) on the contracting and production status of security assistance–related cases and any actual or anticipated problems according to standards and procedures approved jointly by OUSD(A&S) and DSCA.
DSCA lacks visibility into key FMS data housed within other FMS stakeholder systems.	• Amend DoDD 5132.03 and/or DoDD 5105.65 to state that DSCA has the authority to establish a data czar with authorized access into all U.S. government data sources pertaining to FMS cases. The role of the czar is to develop clear guidelines, standards, and incentives for data sharing across the enterprise.
DSCA's SAMM is insufficiently authoritative to ensure that DoD components adhere to its security assistance policies and procedures.	• DoD should elevate the SAMM to the level of a DoD Instruction.
Title 22 gives DoS authority to establish FMS strategic guidance and set priorities for FMS cases, yet DoS is sometimes absent from critical FMS decision points.	• DoS should develop and articulate clear department partner prioritization criteria that align with foreign policy objectives.
Lack of clarity on Title 22 and Title 10 roles and responsibilities can create delays.	• DoS should contribute to FMS-related training and education events to clarify Title 22 authorities and associated roles and responsibilities.
OUSD(P) struggles to crystallize its FMS responsibilities, leading to missed opportunities to streamline competing priorities, reduce confusion, and elevate awareness of how FMS supports U.S. foreign policy and military objectives.	• ASD(SPC) should inform a DSCA-developed standardized FMS prioritization decision tool that incorporates and builds on DoS guidance regarding the partner's role in U.S. strategic planning based on objective criteria. • OUSD(P) should require regional desks to attend the SCEFF prioritization process to increase interagency collaboration.
	• OUSD(P) should encourage CCMDs to integrate partners' FMS-acquired capabilities into operational planning, combined exercise programs, and other opportunities to support the warfighter. • Amend DoDD 5111.01 and/or DoDD 5132.03 to state that OUSD(P)'s authority to establish DoD strategic guidance with respect to foreign partners and allies, to include addressing capability gaps, extends to FMS as well as other security cooperation programs.
OUSD(A&S) lacks responsibility and authority to ensure that MILDEP acquisition officials provide regular and accurate information on the status and scheduling of acquisition contracting and production, including for FMS cases.	• Amend DoDD 5135.02 to state that OUSD(A&S) has the responsibility and authority to develop DoD standards and procedures for reporting information on the status and scheduling of acquisition contracting and production, to ensure this information is readily accessible to DoD acquisition stakeholders, and to conduct periodic evaluations of MILDEP acquisition reporting for accuracy and timeliness.

Table 6.1—Continued

Challenge	Recommendation
USD(R&E) and USD(A&S) lack authority to ensure that exportability is embedded in the MILDEP capability development processes.	• Amend DoDD 5137.02, DoDD 5135.02, and/or DoDD 5132.03 to state that USD (R&E) and USD (A&S) have the authority to ensure that exportability requirements are clearly defined, documented, and resourced by the MILDEPs early in the acquisition lifecycle.
DTSA and ATTR SSG lack authority to make and enforce TSFD decisions related to proposed security assistance cases.	• USD(P) and USD(A&S) should jointly direct research on the trade-offs of establishing a single authority for adjudicating and enforcing decisions throughout (or in certain parts of) the TSFD process.
Air Force and Army FMS case management organizations fall outside the "line authority" of SAF/IA and DASA (DE&C).	• Amend DAFPD 16-1 and AR 12-1 to state that SAF/IA and DASA (DE&C) will participate in the process of selecting top leaders at AFSAC/AFSAT and USASAC, respectively.
SAF/IA, DASA (DE&C), and NIPO lack administrative control over the security assistance activities of MILDEP acquisition organizations.	• Amend DAFPD 16-1, AR 12-1 and the NIPO charter to state that SAF/IA, DASA (DE&C), and NIPO will provide periodic evaluations of MILDEP security assistance and systems command FMS case development and execution performance to their MILDEP leadership, as well as DSCA, USD(P), and USD(A&S).
Duplicative or redundant roles can slow the FMS process; this is a particular issue within Army FMS case management.	• The Army should clarify the duplicative language it uses to describe the roles and responsibilities of the USASAC CPM and the SAMD in DA PAM 12-1. • The Army might consider structural changes to better streamline processes.

Obstacles and Trade-Offs

We are under no illusion that making our proposed RRA changes will be easy or without risk. Nor do we presume all our recommendations will be taken wholesale. The study team's interviews with stakeholders throughout the security assistance community have led us to recognize significant obstacles to altering the constellation of FMS implementation RRAs as a means for improving process performance and effectiveness. We also recognize that some of our recommended changes have been proposed as part of previous FMS reform efforts and either rejected or never implemented, which does not mean they were without merit but does indicate they might again face resistance to being adopted without strong leadership support and institutional follow-through. This section describes these obstacles and some of the trade-offs that DoD leaders would need to consider in deciding the value of a substantial overhaul of security assistance RRAs.

- **There are a multitude of security assistance stakeholders with different interests, perspectives, and priorities.** As described in Chapter 1, within the U.S. government, there are four levels of DoD and DoS organizations with important, at times overlapping, FMS-related roles, including policy and strategy development (OUSD(P), Joint Staff, DoS headquarters), policy and procedural development (DSCA and DTSA), procedural development and planning (MILDEP staffs and secretariats, CCMDs, and embassy missions), and execution (MILDEP case management, contracting and program offices, service component commands, and SCOs). Furthermore, U.S. defense contractors and, of course, foreign partner governments play key roles in FMS case development and execution. And modifying the constellation of FMS RRAs within DoD would inevitably increase or decrease the authorities and responsibilities of some organizations at the expense of others while likely also altering the way in which FMS cases are initiated, prioritized, and managed. For example, increasing DSCA's authority over the SCO workforce and service IAs will mean reducing the authority, respectively, of CCMD commanders and MILDEP secretaries in certain respects, and the latter can be expected to object to such changes unless a strong case can be made to DoD leadership that enhancing DSCA authority to enable FMS efficiency and effectiveness is a priority security objective.

- **There are accountability disconnects at several levels of the security assistance enterprise.** Not only is the organizational structure that governs FMS implementation complex and multilayered, but higher-level organizations (e.g., DSCA and USD[A&S]) that provide FMS-related policy guidance and oversight to intermediate-level organizations (e.g., MILDEP staffs and secretariats) do not necessarily have line authority over the latter's leaders and staff members; likewise, execution organizations (e.g., MILDEP security assistance and acquisition commands) do not always have a direct reporting relationship with MILDEP international affairs secretariats (i.e., DASA [DE&C], SAF/IA, and NIPO). As this report has described, accountability disconnects can frustrate the ability of senior security assistance officials, with the responsibility for ensuring positive FMS outcomes, from directing the FMS activities of lower-level organizations or taking quick corrective action when significant problems arise with respect to FMS implementation. To mitigate the impact of these disconnects, the study team has recommended increasing the authority of higher-level DoD security assistance organizations (e.g., DSCA and the service international affairs secretariats) through such measures as giving them input into the selection of leaders in lower-level security assistance organizations and providing them the opportunity to periodically evaluate these organizations' performance. However, this represents an indirect approach to dealing with a basic organizational dilemma: there is no integrated structure that links security cooperation components in a top-to-bottom hierarchy of singular command-and-control relationships. So, organizations at different levels will inevitably have multiple masters with greater or lesser amounts of authority depending on their areas of responsibility.
- **Some of our recommendations risk slowing, rather than speeding up, the FMS process.** We take the point raised by several stakeholders that increasing the number of organizations at the decisionmaking table for leadership selections and performance evaluations may have unintended consequences that layer in time-consuming bureaucratic steps. As a result, we ultimately tempered our recommendation regarding SCO chief positions to include only those locations where FMS or other security cooperation or security assistance activities have a predominant role in achieving strategic objectives.

We leave the adjudication of those locations to DSCA, the services, and CCMDs, which understand the requirements more than we have the time and resources to discern.

- **Security assistance has not been a focus area for the MILDEPs and their acquisition communities.** Since the Goldwater-Nichols Act reorganized DoD in the mid-1980s, the main purpose of the military departments has been to organize, train, and equip personnel for the CCMDs. From an acquisition standpoint, this has meant developing and fielding defense capabilities to be employed by U.S. forces in operations directed against major U.S. adversaries. The MILDEPs' focus has not been on developing capabilities to be employed primarily by U.S. allies and partners against their adversaries. Accordingly, security assistance was viewed by the services in large part as a means of bolstering the U.S. defense industrial base and alleviating the cost to the U.S. government of developing and procuring advanced weaponry for U.S. forces. Nowhere in service guidance was it stated that a major goal of the U.S. Army, Air Force, or Navy was to help ensure that the militaries of allies and partners were properly equipped so that they might better interoperate with the U.S. military in future conflicts or combat mutual threats on their own, albeit with our support.

  Russia's war against Ukraine and the perceived need to reinforce Taiwan's defenses in the face of an increasing Chinese security threat have begun to shift the perspective of some in the U.S. national security community toward the pre–World War II notion of the United States as providing an "arsenal of democracy" intended to service the defense needs of embattled allies as well as our own. Nevertheless, placing security assistance on par with domestic defense needs would require a profound change in U.S. military culture and doctrine fostered by senior military and civilian leaders over a prolonged period. Consequently, modifications to security assistance RRAs in DoDDs and service regulations would likely not be enough in themselves to shift MILDEP equipping priorities in the direction of allies and partners.
- **DoD's own reluctance to envision allies and partners—and the FMS-supported security assistance provided to them—as critical components of its warfighting contingency planning process is another barrier.** An effective and efficient FMS process requires a culture of appreciation for what capable allies and partners, enabled through the purchase of U.S. defense weapons and systems, bring to the war fight. The 2022 National Defense Strategy highlights allies and partners as a "center of gravity,"[2] and in at least some cases, U.S. military planners appear to recognize how FMS can contribute to this national security strategy. Still, military planners are reluctant to rely too heavily on the contributions of allies and partners.
- **The traditional bottom-up security assistance process is at odds with top-down FMS initiatives.** Historically, most FMS requests filtered up from the bottom of the security assistance bureaucracy. In other words, allied and partner government officials—often in collaboration with U.S. defense industry representatives, U.S. embassy SCOs, and

[2] DoD, 2022, p. 2.

service component commands—presented LORs to MILDEP security assistance CMs, who coordinated the transformation of LORs into LOAs that could pass muster with higher-level U.S. and foreign government officials. Of course, there have been many instances since the formalization of the FMS process in the 1960s and 1970s when foreign partners have circumvented normal channels and presented their requests directly to senior officials in various DoD organizations, as well as to administration and congressional officials, in the hope that gaining their support would convince the MILDEPs to focus on providing what the partner was asking for. More recently, however, the security assistance process has been partially turned on its head to ensure that the provision of military equipment and training to allies and partners is meeting U.S. national security objectives.

During the period of the United States' global war on terrorism, a raft of security cooperation programs were created for the purpose of building the capacity of partners with inadequate means to combat violent, often internationally inspired and supported, extremist groups within their countries and regions. Unlike previous security assistance programs, these BPC programs were primarily managed by DoD, although DoS had an approval role in some, and were explicitly designed to help build partner capabilities that the U.S. government thought were desirable from its national security perspective rather than the partner government's. To this point, however, the partner-centric FMS requirements development and request process has remained separate from BPC planning and programming, though DoD "train and equip" programs make use of the FMS apparatus for executing what are known as "pseudo-FMS" cases. Still, with the increased attention given to allies and partners in U.S. national security strategy, top-level DoD officials are beginning to call for greater integration of Title 10 (DoD) security cooperation and Title 22 (DoS) security assistance programs so as to more effectively use these tools in combination to achieve CCMD objectives at the country and regional levels.

While this makes strategic sense from a DoD perspective, this top-down, U.S. national security–focused approach to security assistance and cooperation is at odds with the traditional FMS process, which is bottom up, partner-centric, and foreign policy oriented. From an RRA standpoint, this means that increasing the authority or responsibility of DoD officials to direct FMS proposals and cases in furtherance of U.S. national security goals is likely to face opposition from FMS stakeholders in the U.S. government and partner nations who hold traditional views of security assistance aims and implementation procedures.

- **The complexity of the FMS process militates against centralized management.** In previous chapters, we have argued that additional authority and responsibility for DoD officials within leading security assistance organizations offers the promise of increased strategic focus, transparency, accountability, and efficiency with respect to FMS implementation. However, the complicated mix of FMS-related organizations and subprocesses, each with its own requirements for operational, technical, and regional expertise, seems to indicate that a degree of caution is warranted when calling for greater centralization of the security assistance enterprise. For example, many of our interviewees bemoaned the slowness and opaqueness of the TSFD process, claiming that it was responsible for a majority of the bottlenecks in FMS case development. Furthermore, some blamed this situation on the lack of an integrated TSFD structure with an organization at the top with clear decisionmaking authority. However, there are reasons why a centralized TSFD authority has yet to emerge within DoD. Put simply, TSFD decisionmaking is complicated. It involves multiple information and technology "owners," representing various DoD components, as well as multiple service and defense agency proponents seeking TSFD approval for multiple informational and technological elements of multiple FMS cases—all managed through a hydra-shaped mechanism of procedural "pipes," coordinating bodies, and approving authorities.

Although DTSA is currently responsible for overseeing and facilitating TSFD, it lacks the capacity, and despite its strong bench of technical experts, it probably lacks the capability to take charge of the whole process. Some FMS stakeholders are skeptical that a single organization can fairly adjudicate the full range of TSFD issues associated with FMS cases developed by other agencies through extended periods of negotiation and requirements determination. This is not to say that it is wrong to give DTSA or other leading security assistance organizations more authority over the processes for which they are nominally responsible; but it will be important to recognize and define the limits of their expanded authority.

In sum, the existence of the obstacles described here mean that DoD could face trade-offs when considering whether to make the significant changes to FMS-related RRAs that we have recommended. For example,

- bureaucratic resistance from FMS stakeholders whose authorities or responsibilities could be diminished and whose interests and expertise might thereby be discounted
- a need for additional resources for personnel to increase the capacity and capability cap of organizations gaining more authority and responsibility
- a narrower conception of FMS needs than a bottom-up requirements process with multiple contributors might produce
- the movement of partners from an FMS approach to meeting their security force training and equipment needs to a direct commercial sales approach that might offer them more control over their defense purchases or even to external suppliers with a more customer-centric approach.

Increasing the importance of security assistance in operational and acquisition decisionmaking to help ensure that allies and partners are more capable to fight alongside U.S. forces or even in lieu of U.S. forces could entail risks, such as the following:

- Allies and partners on which the United States has begun to rely militarily might not "show up" when needed to help combat an important threat to our national security interests.

- The focus on building allied and partner capacity might divert resources from U.S. force development activities at a time when readiness is a big challenge for DoD.

Additionally, greater involvement by DSCA and the service secretariats in selecting and evaluating the leaders of FMS implementing organizations under the line authority of other commands could create confusion over the priority that should be accorded to the initiatives and requests of multiple superiors as well as dilute the control that the MILDEPs have traditionally exercised over personnel management.

Next Steps

To help reduce the salience of the obstacles to FMS RRA changes and the pain of the tradeoffs required to enact them, we recommend that senior leaders in OSD and DSCA with overall responsibility for the ongoing FMS reform effort take the following steps:

1. Take the time to socialize proposed RRA changes with major FMS stakeholders, especially MILDEPs and CCMDs, which might view some of these changes as diminishing their current authorities and responsibilities.
2. Set aside resources to pilot study capability and capacity requirements of proposed RRA changes, and proceed in stages when establishing these changes to gauge the impact of RRA changes on FMS performance.
3. Emphasize to the DoD security assistance community the importance of improving FMS data collection and analysis to discern where FMS implementation problems are most acute and where RRA changes might be most needed to overcome bottlenecks.
4. Treat DoS as an ally rather than an adversary in FMS reform efforts—for example, by including its representatives in working-level discussions regarding proposed RRA changes affecting FMS implementation.
5. Make use of the new Continuous Improvement Process Board as a forum for guiding and monitoring RRA changes as well as discussing and communicating their impact.

APPENDIX

Authorities

FMS are primarily governed by several key authorities and legal frameworks within the U.S. government. These authorities establish the rules and regulations that guide FMS transactions. The primary authorities are outlined in Table A.1.

TABLE A.1

Foreign Military Sales–Related Legal, Policy, and Guidance Documents (Enterprise-Wide)

Legal, Policy, or Guidance Document	Purpose of the Document
Arms Export Control Act	The primary legal framework that authorizes the U.S. government to engage in the export of defense articles and services, including through the FMS program. It establishes the legal basis for arms sales and sets out licensing requirements, procedures, and restrictions.
Foreign Assistance Act	Provides the legislative authority for U.S. foreign assistance programs, including security assistance and military sales. It encompasses various provisions related to the FMS process and defines the scope and purpose of U.S. military assistance.
National Security Memorandum 18, United States Conventional Arms Transfer Policy	Establishes the executive branch's priorities and rationale for adjudicating the export of conventional arms.
DoDD 5132.03, *DoD Policy and Responsibilities Relating to Security Cooperation*	Sets forth guidelines and delineates duties and responsibilities for the management of security cooperation.
Department of Defense Joint Publication 3-20, *Security Cooperation*	Outlines the policies and doctrine governing security cooperation activities. The publication defines the concept of security cooperation and serves as a reference for military personnel and other stakeholders involved in planning, executing, and assessing security cooperation programs and initiatives intended to build the capacity and capabilities of partner nations' security forces, including FMS.
Defense Security Cooperation Agency, *DSCA Manual 5105.38-M: Security Assistance Management Manual* (SAMM)	A key policy document issued by DSCA. It provides detailed guidance and procedures for administering security assistance programs, including FMS. The SAMM outlines the roles and responsibilities of various stakeholders, acquisition processes, pricing methodologies, and other relevant information.

Table A.1—Continued

Legal, Policy, or Guidance Document	Purpose of the Document
Defense Acquisition Guidebook	Provides guidance on the acquisition process within DoD. It includes information on planning, budgeting, contracting, and program management. While not specific to FMS, it may contain relevant information for implementing FMS cases.
International Traffic in Arms Regulations	A set of U.S. regulations that controls the export and import of defense-related articles and services. It outlines the requirements for obtaining licenses, the transfer of technical data, and the classification of defense articles. Compliance with the regulations is crucial in FMS cases involving the transfer of sensitive military technology.

Specific Department of Defense Roles, Responsibilities, and Authorities

While the documents mentioned above provide general guidance, detailed DoD FMS implementation responsibilities and procedures are outlined in department- and agency-specific directives, instructions, and manuals. These are listed in Table A.2.

TABLE A.2

Detailed Department of Defense Foreign Military Sales Implementation Documents

Legal, Policy, or Guidance Document	Purpose of the Document
U.S. Code, Title 10, Section 384, Armed Forces; Chapter 16, Security Cooperation	Establishes the Security Cooperation Workforce Development Program within DOD to be managed by DSCA
DoDD 5105.65, *Defense Security Cooperation Agency*, 2013	Defines the mission, organization and management, responsibilities and functions, relationships, and authorities of DSCA
DoDD 5111.01, *Under Secretary of Defense for Policy (USD(P))*, 2020	Establishes the responsibilities and functions, relationships, and authorities of USD(P)
DoDD 5135.02, *Under Secretary of Defense for Acquisition and Sustainment*, 2020	Establishes the position, responsibilities and functions, relationships, and authorities of USD(A&S)
DoDD 5137.02, *Under Secretary of Defense for Research and Engineering*, 2020	Establishes the position, responsibilities and functions, relationships, and authorities of USD(R&E)
DoDD 5105.72, *Defense Technology Security Administration*, 2016	Defines the mission, organization and management, responsibilities and functions, relationships, authorities, and administration of DTSA
AR 12-1, *Security Assistance, Training, and Export Policy*, 2021	Provides guidance on the execution of FMS cases by the U.S. Army; outlines the responsibilities, procedures, and authorities for conducting FMS activities; and includes information on case development, pricing, procurement, logistics, and financial management

Table A.2—Continued

Legal, Policy, or Guidance Document	Purpose of the Document
DA PAM 12-1, *Security Assistance Procedures and Operations*, 2016	Outlines the responsibilities, procedures, and authorities for conducting FMS activities and includes information on case development, pricing, procurement, logistics, and financial management
Air Force Manual 16-101, *Security Cooperation (SC) and Security Assistance (SA) Management*, 2018	Provides guidance and procedures for implementing security assistance policies within the U.S. Air Force
DAFPD 16-1, *Operations Support: Security Cooperation*, 2021	Establishes the policies and procedures for administering security cooperation programs, including FMS, within the U.S. Air Force and covers the planning, coordination, execution, and oversight of FMS cases
Headquarters Air Force Mission Directive 1-16, *Special Management*, 2022	Establishes the mission, organizational relationships, responsibilities, and delegations of authority/assignments of responsibility of SAF/IA
NIPOI 4920.3, *Implementation of Foreign Military Sales Case Standard Level of Service Policy Guidance*, 2014	Establishes Standard Level of Service Policy for developing and executing Department of the Navy and U.S. Coast Guard FMS cases
Department of the Navy, *Charter for the Deputy Assistant Secretary of the Navy (International Programs) and Director (Navy International Programs Office)*, 2007	Defines the missions, functions, authority, and responsibility of the Deputy Assistant Secretary (International Programs) and director of NIPO

Abbreviations

AECA	Arms Export Control Act
AFSAC	Air Force Security Assistance and Cooperation Directorate
AFSAT	Air Force Security Assistance Training Squadron
AMC	Army Materiel Command
AR	Department of the Army Regulation
ASA (ALT)	Assistant Secretary of the Army (Acquisition, Logistics and Technology)
ASAE	Army Security Assistance Enterprise
ASD	Assistant Secretary of Defense
ASD(SPC)	Assistant Secretary of Defense for Strategy, Plans and Capabilities
ATTR SSG	Arms Transfer and Technology Release Senior Steering Group
BPC	building partner capacity
CCM	country case manager (Army)/command country manager (Air Force)
CCMD	combatant command
CD	country director
CM	case manager
CPD	country program director
CPM	country program manager
DAFPD	Department of the Air Force Policy Directive
DA PAM	Department of the Army Pamphlet
DASA (DE&C)	Deputy Assistant Secretary of the Army for Defense Exports and Cooperation
DoD	U.S. Department of Defense
DoDD	Department of Defense Directive
DoS	U.S. Department of State
DSCA	Defense Security Cooperation Agency
DSCU	Defense Security Cooperation University
DTSA	Defense Technology Security Administration
FMS	Foreign Military Sales
FY	fiscal year
GAO	U.S. Government Accountability Office
GP	Office of the Secretary of Defense—Global Partnerships
IA	implementing agency

IPM	international program manager
LCMC	Life Cycle Management Command
LM	line manager
LOA	Letter of Offer and Acceptance
LOE	line of effort
LOR	Letter of Request
MAJCOM	U.S. Air Force Major Command
MILDEP	Military Department
NDAA	National Defense Authorization Act
NIPO	Navy International Programs Office
NIPOI	Navy International Programs Office Instruction
OSD	Office of the Secretary of Defense
OSD-P	Office of the Secretary of Defense—Policy
OUSD(A&S)	Office of the Under Secretary of Defense for Acquisition and Sustainment
OUSD(P)	Office of the Under Secretary of Defense for Policy
OUSD(R&E)	Office of the Under Secretary of Defense for Research and Engineering
PEO	program executive office
RRA	roles, responsibilities, and authorities
SA	security assistance
SAF/IA	Secretary of the Air Force International Affairs
SAMD	Security Assistance Management Directorate
SAMM	Security Assistance Management Manual
SAPM	Security Assistance Program Manager
SATFA	Army Security Assistance Training Field Activity
SC	security cooperation
SCEFF	Security Cooperation Execution Focus Forum
SCO	security cooperation organization
SCRTF	Security Cooperation Reform Task Force
SDO/DATT	Senior Defense Official and Defense Attaché
SECDEF	Secretary of Defense
SYSCOM	U.S. Navy Systems Command
TSFD	Technology Security and Foreign Disclosure
USACE	U.S. Army Corps of Engineers
USASAC	U.S. Army Security Assistance Command

USD(A&S)	Under Secretary of Defense for Acquisition and Sustainment
USD AT&L	Office of the Under Secretary of Defense for Acquisition, Technology, and Logistics
USD(P)	Under Secretary of Defense for Policy
USD(R&E)	Office of the Under Secretary of Defense for Research and Engineering

References

Air Force Manual 16-101, *Security Cooperation (SC) and Security Assistance (SA) Management*, Department of the Air Force, 2018.

AR—*See* Department of the Army Regulation.

Assistant Secretary of the Navy for RDA, "ASN(RDA) Overall Structure," webpage, undated. As of April 2, 2024:
https://www.secnav.navy.mil/rda/pages/ASNRDAorgchart.aspx

Cronk, Terri Moon, "DoD Restructures Its Acquisition, Technology, Logistics Organization," DoD News, March 29, 2018. As of April 2, 2024:
https://www.defense.gov/News/News-Stories/Article/Article/1479909/dod-restructures-its-acquisition-technology-logistics-organization/

DAFPD—*See* Department of the Air Force Policy Directive.

DA PAM—*See* Department of the Army Pamphlet.

Defense Federal Acquisition Regulation Supplement PGI 204.6, *Contracting Reporting*, effective date February 15, 2024. As of April 2, 2024:
https://www.acquisition.gov/dfarspgi/pgi-204.6-contract-reporting

Defense Federal Acquisition Regulation Supplement PGI 225.73, *Acquisition for Foreign Military Sales*, effective date February 15, 2024. As of April 2, 2024:
https://www.acquisition.gov/dfarspgi/pgi-225.73-acquisitions-foreign-military-sales

Defense Security Cooperation Agency, "Foreign Military Sales FAQ," website, undated. As of April 3, 2024:
https://www.dsca.mil/foreign-military-sales-faq

Defense Security Cooperation Agency, *DSCA Manual 5105.38-M: Security Assistance Management Manual*, Department of Defense, 2012. As of April 4, 2024:
https://samm.dsca.mil/

Defense Security Cooperation University, "History," website, undated. As of January 23, 2024:
https://www.dscu.edu/about/documents/about-docs/courses

Defense Technology Security Administration, "Who We Are: Our Mission," webpage, Office of the Secretary of Defense, undated. As of April 4, 2024:
https://www.dtsa.mil/SitePages/default.aspx

Department of Defense Directive 1403.1, *The Senior Executive Service and Equivalent-Level Positions and Personnel*, October 18, 1982.

Department of Defense Directive 5100.01, *Functions of the Department of Defense and Its Major Components*, Department of Defense, December 21, 2010, incorporating change 1, September 17, 2020. As of April 3, 2024:
https://www.esd.whs.mil/portals/54/documents/dd/issuances/dodd/510001p.pdf

Department of Defense Directive 5105.65, *Defense Security Cooperation Agency*, Department of Defense, October 26, 2012, revised March 2, 2013.

Department of Defense Directive 5105.72, *Defense Technology Security Administration*, Department of Defense, April 26, 2016.

Department of Defense Directive 5111.01, *Under Secretary of Defense for Policy (USD(P))*, Department of Defense, June 23, 2020.

Department of Defense Directive 5111.21, *Arms Transfer and Technology Release Senior Steering Group and Technology Security and Foreign Disclosure Office*, Department of Defense, October 14, 2014. As of April 3, 2024:
https://www.esd.whs.mil/Portals/54/Documents/DD/issuances/dodd/511121p.pdf

Department of Defense Directive 5132.03, *DoD Policy and Responsibilities Relating to Security Cooperation*, Department of Defense, December 29, 2016.

Department of Defense Directive 5135.02, *Under Secretary of Defense for Acquisition and Sustainment*, Department of Defense, July 15, 2020.

Department of Defense Directive. 5137.02, *Under Secretary of Defense for Research and Engineering*, Department of Defense, July 15, 2020

Department of Defense Instruction 5000.85, *Major Capability Acquisition*, Department of Defense, August 6, 2020, revised November 4, 2021. As of April 3, 2024:
https://www.esd.whs.mil/Portals/54/Documents/DD/issuances/dodi/500085p.pdf

Department of Defense Joint Publication 3-20, *Security Cooperation*, Joint Chiefs of Staff, September 9, 2022.

Department of the Air Force Policy Directive 16-1, *Operations Support: Security Cooperation*, February 5, 2021.

Department of the Air Force Mission Directive 1-16, Special Management, September 13, 2022.

Department of the Army Pamphlet 12-1, *Security Assistance Procedures and Operations*, Headquarters, Department of the Army, 2016.

Department of the Army Regulation 12-1, *Security Assistance, Training and Export Policy*, Headquarters, Department of the Army, 2021.

Department of the Navy, *Charter for the Deputy Assistant Secretary of the Navy (International Programs) and Director (Navy International Programs Office)*, December 13, 2007.

Department of the Navy, *NAVYIPOINST 4920.1D: Foreign Military Sales Case Development Manual*, Department of the Navy, 2021.

DoDD—*See* Department of Defense Directive.

Federal Acquisition Regulation, UCF 15.204-2, Part I—The Schedule, effective date February 23, 2024. As of April 2, 2024:
https://www.acquisition.gov/far/15.204-2

Kurilla, Michael, "Statement for the Record General Michael 'Erik' Kurilla Commander, U.S. Central Command Before the Senate Armed Services Committee on the Posture of U.S. Central Command," U.S. Central Command, March 13, 2023. As of April 13, 2024:
https://www.armed-services.senate.gov/imo/media/doc/Kurilla_SASC_Posture_Final_141200March2023.pdf

National Security Memorandum 18, "Memorandum on United States Conventional Arms Transfer Policy," February 23, 2023. As of April 3, 2024:
https://www.whitehouse.gov/briefing-room/presidential-actions/2023/02/23/memorandum-on-united-states-conventional-arms-transfer-policy/

Navy International Programs Office Instruction 4920.3, *Implementation of Foreign Military Sales Case Standard Level of Service Policy Guidance*, Department of the Navy, December 12, 2014.

NIPOI—*See* Navy International Programs Office Instruction.

Navy International Programs Office Portal, homepage, undated. As of April 4, 2024:
https://www.secnav.navy.mil/nipo/Pages/default.aspx

Office of the Deputy Assistant Secretary of the Army for Defense Exports and Cooperation, homepage, undated. As of April 4, 2024:
https://www.dasadec.army.mil

Office of the Spokesperson, "FMS 2023: Retooling Foreign Military Sales for an Age of Strategic Competition: Fact Sheet," U.S. Department of State, May 18, 2023. As of April 3, 2024:
https://www.state.gov/fms-2023-retooling-foreign-military-sales-for-an-age-of-strategic-competition/

Paul, Christopher, Michael Nixon, Heather Peterson, Beth Grill, and Jessica Yeats, *The RAND Security Cooperation Prioritization and Propensity Matching Tool*, RAND Corporation, TL-112-OSD, November 6, 2013. As of February 18, 2024:
https://www.rand.org/pubs/tools/TL112.html

Presidential Policy Directive 23, *Fact Sheet: U.S. Security Sector Assistance Policy*, White House, 2013. As of April 3, 2024:
https://obamawhitehouse.archives.gov/the-press-office/2013/04/05/fact-sheet-us-security-sector-assistance-policy

Sanders, Gregory, Nicholas Velazquez, Emily Hardesty, and Audrey Aldisert, "Defense Acquisition Trends 2023: A Preliminary Look," Center for Strategic and International Studies, December 7, 2023. As of April 3, 2024:
https://www.csis.org/analysis/defense-acquisition-trends-2023-preliminary-look

Secretary of the Air Force International Affairs, homepage, undated. As of April 4, 2024:
https://www.safia.hq.af.mil

Select RAND Research on Security Cooperation: 2006–2019, RAND Corporation, CP-A614-3, 2021. As of April 3, 2024:
https://www.rand.org/pubs/corporate_pubs/CPA614-3.html

U.S. Army, *Army Security Assistance Enterprise (ASAE) Reform*, 2023.

U.S. Code, Title 10, Section 382, Execution and Administration of Programs and Activities.

U.S. Code, Title 10, Section 384, Armed Forces; Chapter 16, Security Cooperation.

U.S. Code, Title 10, Section 1705, Department of Defense Acquisition Workforce Development Account.

U.S. Code, Title 10, Section 9014, Office of the Secretary of the Air Force.

U.S. Code, Title 22, Section 2751, Foreign Relations and Intercourse; Chapter 39, Arms Export Control.

U.S. Department of Defense, *National Defense Strategy of the United States of America*, 2022. As of April 3, 2024:
https://media.defense.gov/2022/Oct/27/2003103845/-1/-1/1/2022-NATIONAL-DEFENSE-STRATEGY-NPR-MDR.PDF

U.S. Department of Defense, *National Defense Strategy Implementation: DOD Workforce Needed to Build Capacity of Allies and Partners. Task 4.5.1—Report and Action Plan*, February 7, 2023. Unclassified document provided by the sponsor and not publicly available.

U.S. House of Representatives, *National Defense Authorization Act for Fiscal Year 2024: Conference Report*, December 6, 2023, Section 810, "Updated Guidance on Planning for Exportability Features for Future Programs." As of April 3, 2024:
https://www.congress.gov/118/crpt/hrpt301/CRPT-118hrpt301.pdf

Washington Headquarters Services, "Frequently Asked Questions About DoD Issuance," webpage, U.S. Department of Defense, undated. As of September 3, 2023:
https://www.esd.whs.mil/Portals/54/Documents/DD/iss_process/FAQs.pdf